THE ROMANS
AND THEIR EMPIRE

Trevor Cairns

ART EDITORS BANKS AND MILES

CAMBRIDGE UNIVERSITY PRESS

**Paintings and drawings
by Anna Mieke
Maps by Peter Taylor
Diagrams by Alan Rhodes**

Published by the Syndics of the Cambridge University Press
Bentley House, 200 Euston Road, London NW1 2DB
American Branch: 32 East 57th Street, New York, N.Y. 10022
© Cambridge University Press 1970
Library of Congress Catalogue Card Number: 69–11026
ISBN: 0 521 07227 1
First published 1970
Reprinted with corrections 1973
Reprinted 1975

Typeset by Hazell, Watson and Viney Ltd
Printed in Great Britain by Jarrold and Sons Ltd, Norwich

Illustrations in this volume are reproduced by kind permission
of the following:
front cover, back cover, pp.11, 36, 53, 60, 61, 85, 88, 89, 94,
Trustees of the British Museum; p.9, Edwin Smith; pp.5, 47,
Italian Institute of London; pp.5, 23, 47, 50, 52, 55, Mansell
Collection; p.6, Museo dei Conservatori, Rome; pp.16, 40,
52, E.N.I.T.; p.35, Archiv für Kunst und Geschichte, Berlin;
p.41, Archivio Fotograf. Gall. Musei Vaticano; p.45,
J. Allan Cash; p.46, Suddeutsche Verlag, Munich; p.46,
Yorkshire Museum; p.47, ND–Giraudon, Paris; p.48,
Yugotours Ltd; p.51, Radio Times–Hulton Picture Library;
p.54, Trustees of the Corbridge Excavation Committee; p.54
(Mars Thincsus pillar) Trustees of the Chester Museum,
photograph C. M. Daniels; pp.58, 66, 76, Dr J. K. St Joseph
and the Cambridge University Department of Aerial
Photography; pp.58, 59, 66, 69, 73, 74, 80, 81, 86, Ministry
of Public Buildings and Works; p.63, H. Russell Robinson,
F.S.A.; pp.51, 63, 89, Trustees of the London Museum;
pp.72, 78, 87, Museum of Antiquities of the University and
the Society of Antiquaries of Newcastle upon Tyne; pp.83, 85,
Gorhambury Estates Company; p.83, Aerofilms Ltd; p.83,
Alan Sorrell; pp.84, 85, J. A. Brown; p.96, Giraudon, Paris.
The drawing on page 26 is by H. Russell Robinson, F.S.A.

Contents

1. THE REPUBLIC

How to be a Roman

Everybody can recognize a Roman when he sees one, and that is quite often. We are always seeing them in films or books or papers. They look something like these models. They are soldiers, of course. People seem usually to think of Romans as being soldiers more than anything else. There is some truth in the idea, because the Romans themselves liked to think that they were fine soldiers.

The Romans in the picture are dressed as soldiers, but everybody knows that it is not the dress that makes the man. The Romans had a definite idea of what one of their men should be like.

Here is a list of Roman words. They are so much like English words that you can easily look them up in a dictionary if you do not know them already. (Many of our words today come from Latin, as the Roman language is called.) These words describe the sort of qualities that a Roman was supposed to have.

FIDELITAS	FORTITUDO	GRAVITAS
DISCIPLINA	SEVERITAS	PIETAS

Look them up and think about them. Do you think that a man with these qualities would make a good soldier?

Could men with these qualities build and rule a great empire? Would they need some other qualities as well?

Look again at the picture of the soldiers, and you will see that the armour and weapons of the two men in front are meant to be used. They are not just wearing fancy dress. Look at the photographs. This strong castle has stood for 1,800 years, yet it was not even built as a castle. It was built as the tomb of the Roman Emperor Hadrian.

The Romans had another very important quality. They knew how to make things that would work well and last for a long time.

The story of Rome is a long one. You will see how a small city-state became a great Empire, how the Empire was ruled by the Caesars for hundreds of years, and how at last it broke down. You will see what they did to the peoples they ruled over, like the people of Britain. You will see bad Romans as well as good Romans. The best of the Romans, the men who made Rome great, the men we remember today as the true Romans, were the men who had fortitude, discipline and those other qualities, and who had the practical common sense to make things work.

The colour photograph is of the Castle St Angelo, Rome. Nowadays it is a museum. There have been various ideas about its original appearance, and one is shown in the black and white picture.

Romans liked to recall how their city began. The bronze she-wolf was made in the early republican period, though the twins were not added until nearly 2,000 years later.

below: Whatever we think of the legends, a settlement on hills beside a river crossing makes sense. On the Palatine hill archaeologists have found traces of huts which must have been like the reconstruction shown. They could date from when Romulus is said to have founded the city in 753 BC.

The seven hills of Rome

Esquiline

Caelian

Viminal

Quirinal

Palatine

Capitoline

Aventine

R Tiber

Heroes of early Rome

You have probably heard the famous stories of the early days of Rome, stories about people like Romulus and Remus, or Lucretia, or Horatius. They are some of the most famous stories in the world. Perhaps that is all they are – stories. Even the Roman historian Livy, when he wrote them down, said that nobody could be sure that they were true. But these stories are well worth thinking about, because they are the stories the Romans liked. True or not, they showed how Romans ought to behave. Every story has a moral. Every story is a sort of parable for Romans.

It would be a waste of time to tell you the stories all over again. All we need do is to remind ourselves of them and then think about the lesson that a Roman could learn from each.

How the city began

The twins Romulus and Remus, the founders of Rome, were once nursed by a she-wolf. *Romans are foster-brothers of wolves, and should show the same fierce courage.* Romulus began to build Rome. Remus mocked at him, and at last jumped over the wall of Rome. Romulus killed him on the spot. *If even your twin brother turns against Rome, it is your duty to kill him.*

The first Romans were all men, many of them outlaws. They needed wives, so they carried off women belonging to the Sabine nation. War followed. It was stopped when the women rushed between the armies and called on their husbands and their brothers and fathers to stop fighting. After this, Romans and Sabines became firm friends. *Rome will gladly make a friend and ally of an honourable enemy.*

How the republic began

Many years after the time of Romulus there came bad kings, of the family of Tarquin. One of them brought disgrace upon a noble Roman lady, called Lucretia, who killed herself rather than bear the shame. The Romans rose up and drove out the king and all his family. *A Roman prefers death to dishonour. The Romans are free people, and therefore will not serve a king.*

The Romans appointed two men called consuls to rule over them. One consul, Brutus, discovered a plot to bring back King Tarquin. He sentenced the traitors to death, even though his own sons were among them. *A Roman loves justice and the freedom of Rome even more dearly than his own sons.*

How the republic was defended

Tarquin got the help of the powerful king of the Etruscans. Rome was not ready to fight, but was saved by Horatius, who held a bridge against the whole Etruscan army. When the bridge had been destroyed behind him he refused to surrender, but swam back to Rome in full armour. *A Roman will face any odds for the sake of Rome, and he will never surrender.*

The Etruscan king besieged Rome and looked like starving the Romans out. Some young Romans swore that they would kill him. The first to try, Caius Mucius, was caught by the Etruscans. The king threatened him with torture unless he told all he knew about Rome. Caius showed how little he feared pain by thrusting his hand into a fire until it was burned away. The king admired his bravery so much that he set him free. In return, Caius warned the king that many more Romans would try to kill him soon. The king realized that it was hopeless to try to conquer such people, and made peace with Rome. *Romans despise pain, and will suffer anything for Rome. A Roman will deal honourably with an honourable enemy. Bravery and resolution may win even when everything seems lost.*

Minerva, goddess of wisdom, who gave protection in war. This 8½-inch (22 cm) Etruscan bronze was made about the time when the Tarquins are said to have ruled in Rome.

These are the most famous tales of early Rome. They are not the only ones, but they show you how the Romans expected their heroes to behave. This was the sort of behaviour that a Roman should try to copy.

You may say that these Roman heroes are too good to be true, that they are just not human, that you cannot expect real people to behave like that. Certainly, there were plenty of Romans who did not behave in the least like these heroes, and there were times when it looked as if very few Romans really believed in those qualities we mentioned on page 4. That is true enough. But when you read about some of the things that the Romans really did, not just stories, but fact, you may often be reminded of what we have been thinking about in the last few pages.

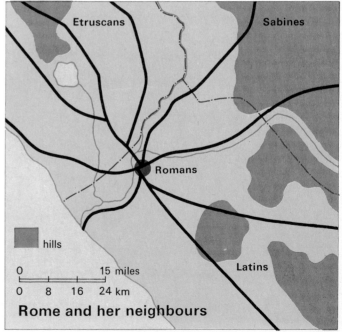

Etruscans

Sabines

Romans

☐ hills

0 _____ 15 miles
0   8   16   24 km

Latins

Rome and her neighbours

From many directions paths, later replaced by roads, converged on Rome.

S.P.Q.R.

Nowadays, if I were to see the letters O.H.M.S. stamped on anything – an envelope, for instance – I should know that it had something to do with the government. The letters stand for 'On Her Majesty's Service', because we in Britain still have a king or queen as the chief person in our country. The Romans had a set of letters, too, for anything that belonged to the state. The Roman letters were S.P.Q.R., and they stood for the words 'Senatus Populus Que Romanus'. In English, that means 'The Senate and the People of Rome'. After they had driven out Tarquin in 510 B.C. the Romans were determined to have nothing more to do with kings.

The Roman people, all the free citizens of Rome, would meet together in the main square of the city, which was called the Forum. Here they would listen to speeches and vote on any laws that were suggested. They would also vote for the magistrates whom they wanted to rule over them each year. So you can see how 'People of Rome' gets into S.P.Q.R.

A typical stern Roman. Probably a senator of the late republic.

FORUM

What about 'Senate'? This was a council made up of the chief men of the oldest and most important families in Rome. They were supposed to sit down and think things out in a calm, careful way. Because they had plenty of time, and because they were supposed to be mostly steady and experienced and wise men, they could discuss things far better than a crowd of thousands of citizens standing in the Forum. So the Senate was to give good advice and suggest good laws to the People.

The families whose members sat in the Senate, the 'best' families, were called patricians. The others, the 'common' Romans, were called plebeians.

There were still some jobs which the king had done and which could not be done by a big meeting of the People or by a meeting of the Senate. The king had performed some religious services, had been chief judge and chief general, and had watched over the other magistrates and officers to see that they did their jobs properly. Now that the Romans had decided to have no more kings, who would be able to do these jobs?

It was easy to appoint one man to look after the religious services which the king had done. He was called the 'Sacrificial King'. He simply performed the sacrifices at the altars, and had no other powers.

The other jobs were more of a problem. The Romans were afraid that if they gave all those powers to one man he might become too strong and too ambitious, and try to make himself into a king.

However, the Romans were good at solving practical problems. Instead of appointing one man, they appointed two. They would share the power and jobs which the king used to have, and each would watch the other to make sure that he did not become too powerful. These two men would be changed every year, so there would be even less chance of their grabbing too much power. These men, the two chief men of the Roman republic, were called consuls.

SENATE

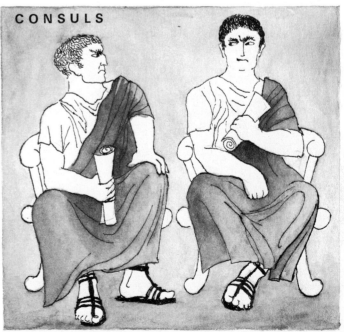

CONSULS

The peasant farmers

The Romans were getting rid of the king and setting up a republic roughly about the time that the Greek city-states were fighting their most famous wars. The Romans, too, were living in a city-state. We do not really know a great deal about this city-state; it was certainly much smaller and poorer than the great city which most of us imagine when the word 'Rome' is mentioned. It may have covered only one or two of the famous Seven Hills, and there would be none of the mighty buildings whose ruins can still be seen. It would be a simple city with people who lived a simple, healthy but hard life.

The Romans lived in the city or on their farms outside. All of them, even the patricians, worked hard on the land. They were near enough to be able to attend their meetings easily. As for war, fighting usually happened in those months of the summer when both the Romans and their enemies could take a few weeks off from farming. There seems to have been some fighting most summers.

These Romans were proud of the sort of things they did. They believed in hard work, hard fighting and honesty. They were poor, and looked down on wealthy merchants. They had a feeling that wealth was likely to make people soft and selfish, and that men who made their living by business deals were likely to be too interested in money. Like the Spartans, the Romans did not trust money.

Patricians and plebeians

There was one serious thing wrong with the Roman republic, which caused trouble time after time for hundreds of years. It was something that nowadays we call 'class distinction', the feeling that some people are 'upper-class' and therefore superior while others are 'lower-class' and therefore inferior.

In Rome, as you know, the Senate was made up of members of the 'old' families, whose ancestors had helped Romulus, so it was said, to found Rome. They had always been leaders. They had taken the lead in driving out the king, and now they ran Rome. The consuls and the other magistrates, as well as the Senate, were all patricians. The plebeians could vote in the Forum, but this was not always enough to protect them if the patricians behaved badly.

Often the patricians behaved very well indeed. Because they were proud of their families, they wanted to live up to the reputation their ancestors had won. They wanted to show that they truly deserved their privileges. But sometimes there were too many patricians who were proud in a very different way, who despised the plebeians and tried to use their power cruelly.

Only fifteen years after the republic had been started there was serious trouble. Because of bad harvests, many plebeian farmers had borrowed money from patricians. Then they had been unable to pay it back. The laws about debt were very severe. Debtors could be put in prison and even sold as slaves. Some of the patricians showed no mercy, not even to men who had been unable to repay because they had been away with the army, fighting for Rome, instead of working their farms. The patricians in the Senate kept on promising to do something to ease the plight of debtors, but broke their promises. At last the plebeians acted. They went on strike.

These plebeians were soldiers as well as farmers, and when they came back from a battle and found that things were as bad as ever, they simply marched out of Rome and made their camp on a hill a couple of miles away. Here they said they would start a new city, and leave the patricians to keep Rome for themselves. Some of the worst of the patricians would have been ready to do this; they thought that Rome would be better empty than full of plebeians. But most of the patricians came to their senses. They sent to the plebeians, asking them to come back and promising this time that there should be two entirely new magistrates who would be plebeians, be elected by the plebeians, protect the plebeians and have full power to do their work properly. These two men would be called 'Tribunes of the People'. The plebeians had won. They did not really want to desert Rome, any more than the patricians wanted to lose so many good men. When the first two tribunes had been appointed the plebeians came back to Rome.

The tribunes were very important men in Rome. At first there were only two, but as the city grew more tribunes were appointed. During his year of office, each tribune was sacred; nobody dared to harm him. A tribune could not *make* laws, but he could *stop* anything that seemed likely to injure any of the plebeians. All he had to do was to say 'Veto!', which is Latin for 'I forbid', and that was the end of that.

This idea of having tribunes worked. Of course, that does not mean that all Romans lived together happily ever after; this is not a fairy story. There were still times when patricians and plebeians hated each other, and sometimes men who were foolish or weak or wicked were elected as tribunes. All the same, the patricians never again drove the plebeians to going on strike. The worst danger to the Roman republic, the danger that Rome would be torn apart from inside, was overcome.

TRIBUNES

The dictator

Danger in war was another thing, and it often threatened Rome. Sometimes the danger was so great that only the quickest and boldest action could save Rome. At such a time the Senate would appoint one man who would have complete power over all the Romans. This man was called a dictator, and it was death to disobey his orders. The dictator would be complete master of Rome until he had saved the city, and then it was his duty to hand back his powers to the consuls, the Senate and the Roman people.

The story of Cincinnatus shows how a dictator was supposed to behave. It happened that one of the Roman consuls had been trapped and surrounded by the enemy, and would soon have to surrender. The position was hopeless. When the Senate heard the news they decided that they must appoint a dictator, and that Cincinnatus was the best man for the job. He was a patrician and had been a consul himself, but he was not a rich man. When the messengers from the Senate came to him, he was busy ploughing on his farm. The messengers told him that the Senate had appointed him dictator for six months. At once he collected together the men still in Rome – mostly men who had been too old or too young to be with the army. With these as his soldiers, he marched quickly to where the enemy was surrounding the Roman army. Quietly, by night, Cincinnatus and his men surrounded the enemy. When daylight came, the enemy found themselves caught between two Roman armies; attacked from both sides, the enemy surrendered. The dictator had turned a disaster into a great victory. He returned to Rome and gave back his powers to the Senate, after being dictator for only a fortnight. Then he returned to his farm and got on with the ploughing.

That story, like many of the stories of early Rome, may or may not be completely true. But the Romans used to think of Cincinnatus as the perfect example of a dictator.

From city-state to Empire

Rome begins to spread

We have been thinking so far about a little city-state where most of the peasant-citizens led a hard, simple life, farming and fighting. Within 250 years of the founding of the republic, the city of Rome was mistress of the whole of Italy. It did not happen suddenly, and the Romans did not deliberately set out to conquer the whole of Italy; they did not even start wars. The Romans spread their power over Italy because once they did get into a war they never let themselves be beaten. And when a war was over they were often able to persuade their enemies that they would be better off with Rome.

You know enough about the Romans already to be able to understand that they were very dogged fighters. They did not always win their battles, and their generals were not always very clever. The Roman soldiers, though, always fought very hard. Even if they were beaten in one or two battles, they would come back at their enemies until at last they won.

Winning a war is one thing. Making a good peace is another, and it is usually much more difficult. The really hard thing is to get the loser to agree with what the winner wants, and not go on being an enemy waiting for a chance of revenge. The Romans were better than most people – the Greeks, for example – at making friends of their enemies, just as they had done with the Sabines, according to the old tale we mentioned on page 7. Often the Romans would ask their defeated enemies to become their allies, and to help Rome in any war against anybody else. These allies would go on ruling their own cities as they always had done, and they would be given special rights in Rome itself, though they would not be full Roman citizens.

It did not always work. Sometimes old enemies only pretended to become allies, and waited for a chance to fight Rome again. Sometimes the Romans were foolish and offended their allies. On the whole, though, the Romans had a good sense of fair play, and treated their allies justly. As you will see, the time would come when Rome was in such trouble that only the loyalty of her allies saved her.

Another thing that the Romans often did when they had won a war was to found a colony. A Roman colony was nothing like a Greek colony; in fact, it was nearly the opposite. The Romans would take enough land for a city and its farms. Then a force of Roman soldiers would march off to this land, build houses and make farms, and live in the new city. These soldiers were of course full citizens of Rome, and they remained Roman citizens. They could return to Rome and vote in the elections, for instance, whenever they wished. By planting

colonies like this, the Romans could feel that they had a force of their own people living among their new allies. These colonists could be relied on to try to keep the allies loyal to Rome and, if things went wrong, to fight for Rome.

Colonies were also very useful as a method of finding land for the extra people as the population grew. This seems to have been almost the only way in which Roman and Greek ideas about colonies were alike.

During the 250 years between the founding of the republic and Rome's becoming mistress of Italy, the Romans fought many enemies, and often had a very bad time before they won. One of the worst times was in 390 B.C., when the Gauls, wild, strong barbarians from north of the Alps, poured into Italy. The Gauls beat the Roman army and destroyed all the city except the citadel on the Capitol Hill. That was when the senators, refusing to go to the Capitol where they would be useless mouths, remained in the deserted and doomed city, sitting silently until the Gauls rushed in and killed them. At last the Romans had to pay much gold to the Gauls before they would go away. But, as you know, the Romans would never accept defeat. Soon they fought the Gauls again, and

beat them. The Gauls retired far from Rome, and settled in the valley of the River Po.

Most of the time Rome fought with other cities and peoples in central Italy – Latins, Etruscans, Aequians, Volscians, Samnites. Sooner or later, the Romans always won. The Romans were lucky in one thing: their enemies usually fought them one at a time, so that Rome was never completely overwhelmed by numbers. Bit by bit, Italy came under the control of Rome, as the map will show you. By 280 B.C. the Romans were coming up against the rich Greek cities of southern Italy, those cities which had grown from the colonies founded by the Greeks hundreds of years before.

A quarrel broke out between Rome and the Greek city of Taras, or Tarentum. The men of Tarentum knew that Rome was too strong for them, so they asked for help in Greece. It was now more than forty years after the death of Alexander the Great, and his great empire had been cut up between generals who made themselves kings. There was now a young king living in a kingdom to the north of Greece who was known to be a good general. His name was Pyrrhus and his kingdom was called Epirus. This was the man who came to help Tarentum against Rome.

Pyrrhus had learnt about war from generals who had known Alexander. He was a Hellenistic king, with all the latest ideas and weapons. One of his weapons was a number of huge beasts which terrified the Roman soldiers. These beasts seemed to be some sort of cow, with the two horns growing at the bottom instead of the top of the head. (You can easily guess what they were – a weapon which Alexander had first met in India.) Scattered and trampled down by these huge beasts, the Romans were defeated. Pyrrhus offered them the chance of peace. The Romans refused. In the next battle the Romans were beaten again. Again they refused to make peace.

The temple of Poseidon, Greek god of the sea. It was built in the fifth century BC by the Greek colonists of Poseidonia, which the Romans later renamed Paestum.

Rome's power over the Italian peninsula by 264 BC

Pyrrhus was worried. 'If', he said, 'I win any more battles like that, I shall have lost the war.' His victories were costing him too much, and the Romans could replace their losses more easily than he could. Sure enough, he lost the next battle and had to go home. Now you know what is meant by a 'Pyrrhic victory'. Also you have seen how the Romans won their wars – and this time the story is undoubtedly true. Up to this time we have not been able to feel sure of all the details of Roman history; probably many of the best-known stories are no more than stories. But now that we can be fairly sure of the facts, we see that the Romans really could sometimes live up to their old traditions.

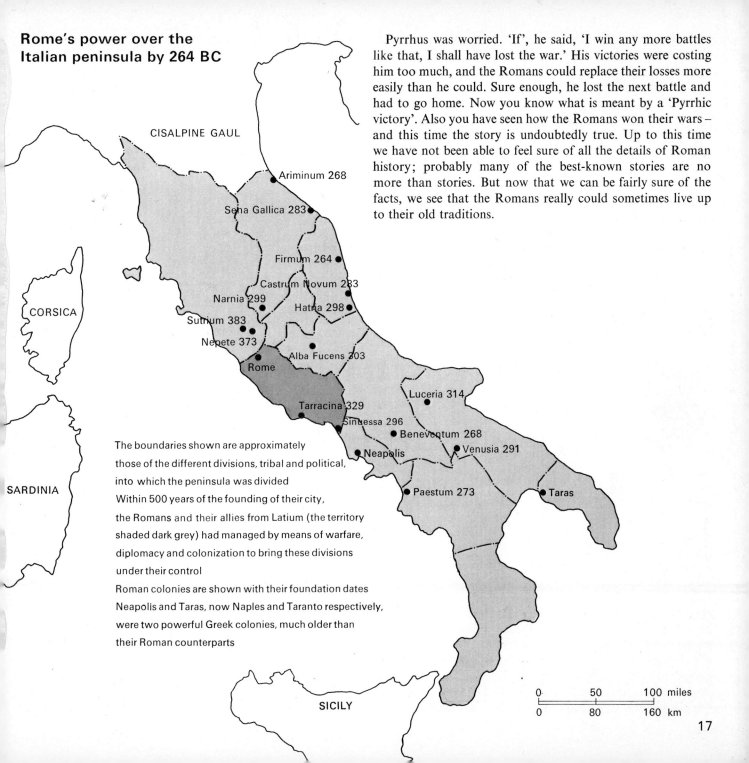

CISALPINE GAUL

CORSICA

SARDINIA

Ariminum 268

Sena Gallica 283

Firmum 264

Castrum Novum 283

Narnia 299
Hatria 298

Sutrium 383

Nepete 373
Alba Fucens 303

Rome

Tarracina 329

Luceria 314

Sinuessa 296

Beneventum 268

Neapolis
Venusia 291

Paestum 273

Taras

SICILY

The boundaries shown are approximately those of the different divisions, tribal and political, into which the peninsula was divided
Within 500 years of the founding of their city, the Romans and their allies from Latium (the territory shaded dark grey) had managed by means of warfare, diplomacy and colonization to bring these divisions under their control
Roman colonies are shown with their foundation dates
Neapolis and Taras, now Naples and Taranto respectively, were two powerful Greek colonies, much older than their Roman counterparts

| 0 | 50 | 100 miles |
| 0 | 80 | 160 km |

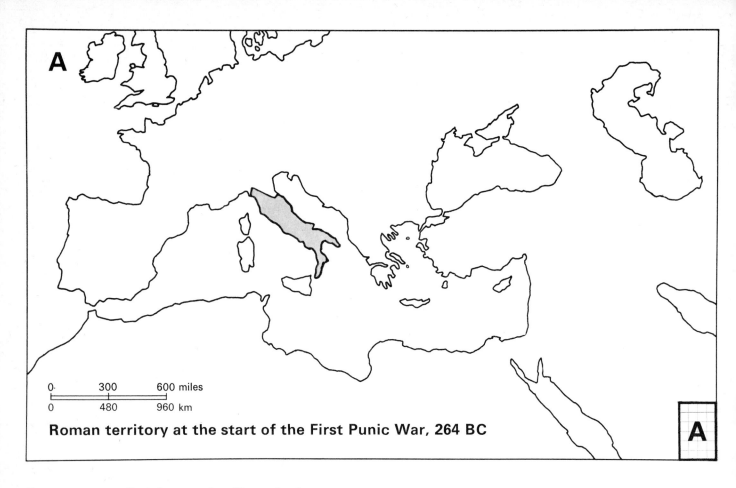

A

Roman territory at the start of the First Punic War, 264 BC

A

Rome versus Carthage: the first clash

A is the first in a series of five maps and graphs which compare the size of Rome's Empire at different times. The others are shown on pages 24, 25, 42 and 43. The graph blocks show the same areas of Roman territory as the maps, arranged to help comparison.

If you look at the first graph and the map above you will see how Rome had spread her power all over the peninsula of Italy. Now if you look at the map opposite you will see what lay to the south of Italy; first the island of Sicily, next the coast of Africa. On the coast of Africa stood the great city of Carthage.

Carthage had been founded hundreds of years earlier by people from Phoenicia, which was why the word Punic, or Phoenician, was sometimes used to describe the people of Carthage. Like all Phoenicians, as you will remember, the

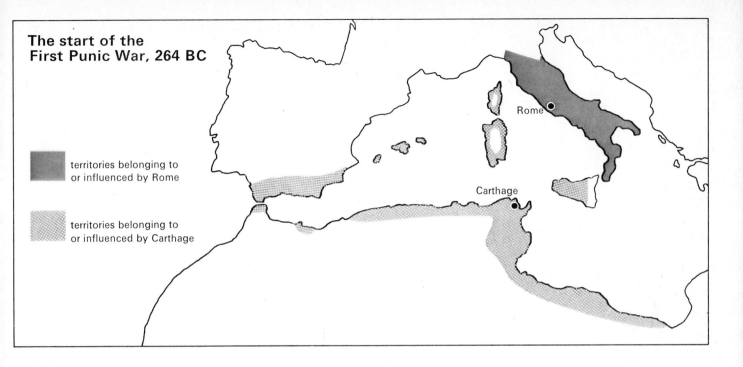

**The start of the
First Punic War, 264 BC**

territories belonging to
or influenced by Rome

territories belonging to
or influenced by Carthage

Rome

Carthage

Carthaginians were very good merchants and sailors. Their merchant ships traded all over the western Mediterranean and even beyond, into the Atlantic; they may even have sailed as far as cold, foggy Britain to trade for tin, which they needed to make copper into bronze. The Punic war-galleys swept these seas, sinking pirates and driving away anyone else who tried to trade there.

As you know, the Romans were farmers, not merchants. They were soldiers, not sailors. There was no reason why the Romans and the Carthaginians should quarrel, because they wanted entirely different things. In fact, Carthage had helped Rome in one or two earlier wars. Yet Rome and Carthage did fight, and these Punic Wars, as they are called, were the wars that turned Rome into a great empire. Before that happened, however, these wars nearly saw the end of Rome.

The quarrel arose because of trouble in Sicily. It was merely a little, local war, until one side appealed for help to Carthage and the other side to Rome. Neither Carthage nor Rome was really involved, but in each city the government felt that it could not afford to look as if it were backing down, as if it were

afraid to protect its friends or allies. So, in 264 B.C., Rome and Carthage went to war.

At first, rather like the Athens-Sparta War two centuries earlier, this was the struggle of the whale and the elephant. The Carthaginians were very strong on the sea, the Romans on the land. Unless the whale could learn to fight on land, or the elephant learn to swim, it looked as though neither side could win.

The elephant learned to swim.

The Romans showed the determination and practical common sense that you may be beginning to expect of them. You will remember from when you learned about the battle of Salamis that galley-warfare needed great skill on the part of captains and rowers. The Romans knew this perfectly, and knew that the Carthaginians would sink their galleys before the Roman sailors could gain experience and skill. On the other hand, if the Romans could manage to avoid being rammed and could get their soldiers aboard the enemy galley, the Roman soldiers would usually be able to beat the soldiers on the Carthaginian vessel. How could this be done? That was the problem.

19

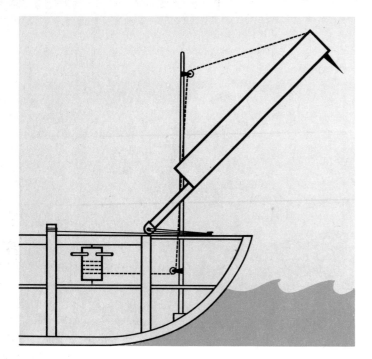

The answer was: a drop-bridge with a big spike. There are no genuine Roman pictures of this weapon, so the diagram only shows how this bridge may have been designed. You can work out for yourself how it could be used, and how it made everything much easier for the Roman captains.

Even with this boarding-bridge, the Romans did not have an easy time. They were still not very skilful at sea, and lost many galleys in storms. The Romans were sometimes defeated on land, too. There was one very clever Carthaginian general called Hamilcar, who did well in Sicily. There was the consul Regulus, who led an army to attack Carthage and was taken prisoner; he died like a hero, eventually, but that did not alter the fact that he had thrown away an entire Roman army. So the war went on for more than twenty years before Carthage admitted defeat.

In 241 B.C. peace was made. Carthage gave up all her claims to Sicily, and Rome took the whole island. Carthage also paid a huge sum of money to Rome.

'Hannibal at the gates!'

Peace had been declared, but neither side meant it. Carthage was still very strong, and wanted her revenge. The great general Hamilcar took an army to Spain, and began to found cities and win over the Spanish tribes until he had given Carthage a new empire in Spain to make up for lost Sicily. One of his cities was called New Carthage, and you will still be able to recognize the name of Carthage if you look at a modern map of Spain. Meanwhile the Romans also knew that this peace was only a truce. The western Mediterranean was not big enough for both Rome and Carthage. Rome was beginning to look outside Italy. While Carthage was taking Spain, Rome took the islands of Sardinia and Corsica. It was merely a matter of time before war broke out again.

The upper map will show you what the position was in 218 B.C., when the struggle began once more. The Second Punic War, as it is called, was begun by the Carthaginian general in Spain, when he deliberately attacked the Greek colony of Saguntum, which had equally deliberately been promised protection by Rome. This general was a young man of twenty-nine, the son of Hamilcar. He had promised his father to carry on the fight with Rome, and his plans were ready. His name was Hannibal.

Hannibal knew that the only way to bring down Rome properly was to beat the Romans in Italy itself. Only that would really destroy Rome's power. It meant that he had to take his army to Italy. Since the First Punic War the Roman navy had been stronger than the Carthaginian navy, so Hannibal could not take his army by sea. That left him only one thing to do. He had to march over land to Italy.

You can see on the map the route which Hannibal took. You probably know already about the really hard part of the march, when he crossed the Alps. It was a terrible march. Hannibal approached the Alps with about 60,000 men. Only about 23,000, exhausted and half-starved, struggled down into the plains of the River Po, in northern Italy.

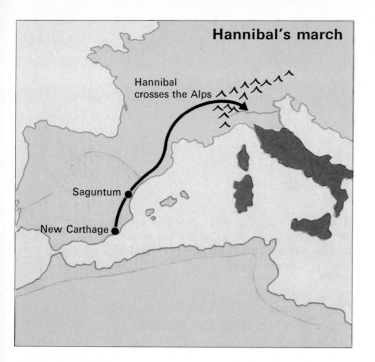

Hannibal's march

Hannibal crosses the Alps

Saguntum

New Carthage

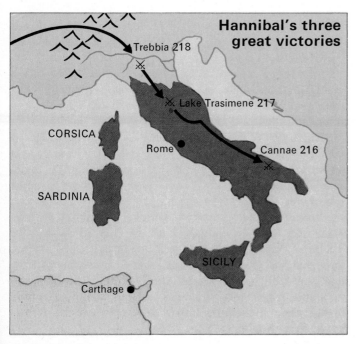

Hannibal's three great victories

Trebbia 218

Lake Trasimene 217

CORSICA

Rome

Cannae 216

SARDINIA

SICILY

Carthage

The Romans had been too slow to catch Hannibal on his way to the Alps, but this seemed better still. Such a weary, miserable wreck of an army would not stand for a moment against the hardy citizen-soldiers of Rome. How could the Romans know that they were facing one of the greatest generals the world has ever known, a general almost as brilliant as Alexander had been?

The lower map shows the lessons the Romans had to learn before they realized quite how good Hannibal was. The story of Hannibal would take a big book. Here we are busy with the story of Rome, and how at last the Romans were too strong even for the great Carthaginian leader. There is room only for an outline of the story.

The first Roman army to fight Hannibal was cut to pieces beside the River Trebbia. This was a blow, but war is full of ups and downs. Next year another big Roman army went to look for Hannibal. Few of the soldiers in it ever came back; most of them, including the consul who led them, were cut down or drowned at the battle of Lake Trasimene.

With two armies slaughtered, some of the Romans began to realize the truth about Hannibal. A dictator was appointed, a man named Fabius. He refused to face Hannibal in battle. Instead, he and his men followed the Carthaginians as they marched into the south of Italy, trying to cut off small parties of them and to prevent them from getting enough food. Every time Hannibal turned on him, Fabius scuttled away into the hills. These 'Fabian tactics', as they were called, were safe, but they were slow. It would be years before they could wear down Hannibal's army. Could Rome afford to wait so long?

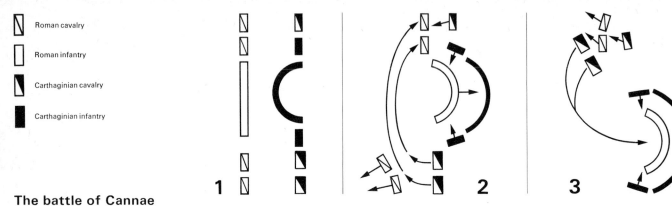

Roman cavalry

Roman infantry

Carthaginian cavalry

Carthaginian infantry

1

2

3

The battle of Cannae

1 Hannibal is stronger in cavalry, weaker in infantry. He makes his infantry seem weaker still, pushed forward in an arch.
2 The Roman infantry advances; the arch bends back — but its sides hold, pressing in on the Roman mass.

Meanwhile Hannibal's cavalry rout the Roman cavalry, first on one wing, then on the other.
3 Crowded together, attacked on all sides, the Roman infantry are destroyed.

In 216 B.C. the Romans sent an army at least three times as big as Hannibal's, under both consuls. You can see from the diagram what happened. The battle of Cannae was the most shocking disaster in Roman history. At the end of the day there lay on the battlefield 76,000 corpses. 6,000 of these were of Hannibal's men; the rest belonged to Rome and her allies.

After a moment of panic, the people of Rome stood firm. One of the consuls, the man who had been mostly to blame for the disaster, had escaped and gathered together a small force of survivors. The Senate did not waste time in blaming him, but thanked him for not having despaired and for trying to save something from the wreck. But when Hannibal sent a message that he was ready to accept ransom for his prisoners, the Senate coldly replied that he could do as he pleased with them. Rome had no use for men who surrendered. This was the spirit in which the Romans carried on with the war. It is hard to decide whether they were more than human, or less.

However you judge them, the Romans certainly kept their heads. Hannibal had hoped that, when he had beaten the Romans so severely, the other peoples of Italy would take this chance of rising up against Rome. He was disappointed. Some did, but most of Rome's allies remained loyal. Now Rome had her reward for being just to her allies. They locked their gates against Hannibal.

The Romans now knew Hannibal's strength; he could win battles. They also spotted his weakness; he still did not have enough men to take a big city like Rome. He did not have the siege engines, he did not have enough soldiers to besiege the city while at the same time collecting food and holding off relieving forces. Hannibal could come to the gates of Rome, and he did. But, as long as the Romans kept cool, he could never force those gates open.

So the Romans went back to Fabian tactics in Italy, wherever Hannibal was. Meanwhile they raised new armies which began to conquer Spain and which began to attack and capture those few cities in Italy and Sicily that had sided with the Carthaginians. Without reinforcements, even the great Hannibal was baffled. Hannibal never received reinforcements. The government of Carthage feared that Hannibal and his family were becoming too powerful, and never made a serious effort to help him. The only man who tried to come to Hannibal's aid was his brother, Hasdrubal, who brought a fresh army from Spain, over the Alps and into northern Italy, in 207 B.C. But Hasdrubal was trapped by large Roman armies, and the first news Hannibal had of his coming was when the Romans one night threw his brother's head into his camp. Still unbeaten, but gradually becoming weaker as the years went by, Hannibal prowled about the south of Italy while, everywhere else, Roman armies were winning the war.

Scipio: a bust probably made in the first century BC.

Terms of Peace

Carthage must give up

one hundred hostages chosen by the Romans;

all Roman prisoners, deserters, runaway slaves;

all lands, except for a small area around the city and a few trading settlements permitted by the Romans;

all but ten warships;

all war elephants;

two hundred talents of silver each year, to be paid to Rome for the next fifty years;

all control over the neighbouring African peoples, who will be allies of Rome.

Carthage must never make war without permission from Rome, and must always help Rome when required.

If they will keep to these terms, the people of Carthage are to be allowed to live freely, according to their own laws.

At last the Romans found a daring general called Scipio who took an army to Africa and began to attack Carthage. The government of Carthage now sent for Hannibal. The ships which had never been able to bring reinforcements came to take him home.

Near Carthage Hannibal fought Scipio. The battle of Zama was his first and last defeat.

The Second Punic War ended in 201 B.C. Carthage had to accept whatever terms Rome would offer. They were hard terms.

Possibly a contemporary bust of Hannibal, found near Capua, an Italian town once allied with him.

Rome's revenge

You know that the Romans had often treated defeated enemies well, and turned them into allies. With Carthage it was different. Rome took from Carthage her Spanish empire, her allies in Africa, her ships and an enormous sum of money. Besides, Carthage had to promise never to build up an army or navy again, and always to obey Rome's orders in any dealings with other peoples or cities; Carthage could never be strong, nor even look for friends, unless Rome gave permission.

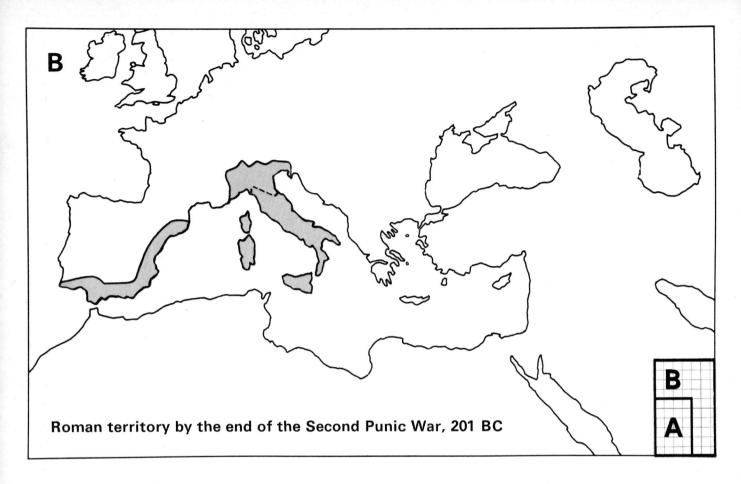

B

Roman territory by the end of the Second Punic War, 201 BC

The Romans were still a little nervous, for Hannibal was still alive and was becoming the leading man in the Carthaginian government. In 195 B.C. the Romans sent envoys to arrest Hannibal and bring him to Rome. Hannibal fled. For some years he was the guest of Greek kings in Asia Minor, but the Romans kept trying to catch him. At last, in despair and weariness, he took poison.

Still there were Romans who were not satisfied. One of them was Cato, a stern, sour man who was constantly telling the Romans how they should behave, and how much better Romans had been in the old days. He was an unpleasant, mean man, but many of the things he said were true, and he did not care if they made him unpopular. Because of this, many Romans believed him. Cato still wanted revenge. When he spoke in the

Senate, whatever the subject being discussed, he always ended with three words: 'Delenda est Carthago.' That means: 'Carthage must be destroyed.'

So the hatred of the Romans for Carthage was not allowed to die away. More than fifty years after the Second Punic War, Rome picked a quarrel with her old enemy. Carthage tried to please Rome by giving way on all points, but the Romans kept making more demands until the Carthaginians realized the truth and, with hopeless bravery, fought. The Third Punic War was simply the siege of Carthage by a big Roman army. Despite a heroic defence, in 146 B.C. the Romans took Carthage –and destroyed it. There remained only a rubble-strewn waste.

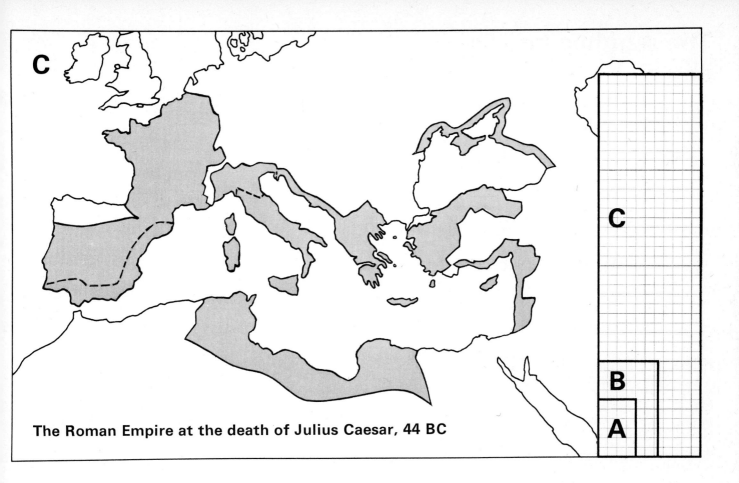

The Roman Empire at the death of Julius Caesar, 44 BC

Eagles over the Mediterranean

These two maps and the graphs which go with them tell the story of how Roman power grew during the century and a half after the Second Punic War. During those years, in war after war, the Roman legions carried their eagle standards to victory. One country after another fell under the power of Rome, until the Romans could call the Mediterranean 'Mare Nostrum' – 'Our Sea'.

It would not be quite fair to blame the Romans for going about conquering other people and building an empire. Part of the fault was the other people's. Rome was so strong that other people sometimes dragged her into their quarrels, in the hope that the Roman army would be of some help to them. But once Rome was called in, she usually stayed.

Another thing to remember is this. The more land Rome got, the more she had to protect against attacks and raids from outside. Sooner or later the Romans would put an end to such attacks by going out and conquering the lands of the attackers. This could go on and on, of course, until something like an ocean or a desert or another mighty empire stopped the legions.

Meanwhile the Empire of Rome went on growing. More and more soldiers needed, more and more lands to conquer and to rule, more and more money to pay for it all. Those simple peasant-citizens who had founded the republic had never thought of anything like this.

The republic breaks down

In the provinces –
soldier, governor, taxman . . .

Soldiers were always needed now. Many legions were kept
busy all the time, winning new lands or defending lands that
were already ruled by Rome. The old-fashioned Roman soldier, who put down his spade and took up his spear for a few
weeks every summer, was no use now. The long wars against
Hannibal in Spain, in Africa, in Greece, in Asia Minor – there
seemed to be no end to the need for legions all over the Mediterranean – forced the Romans to employ full-time soldiers.

As their Empire grew, the Romans were able to bring many of
their new subjects to fight in the Roman army. These soldiers,
though, were only 'auxiliaries' – helpers, second-rate troops.
The backbone of the Roman army was the heavily-armed foot
soldier of the legion. The legionary, as he was called, had to be a
Roman citizen. He signed on for about twenty years' service with
the eagles, and he was very well trained and equipped. After
the great general Marius had reorganized the army, round about
100 B.C., the Roman legionary was a real professional, very
highly skilled and fairly well paid. The picture shows you one
of these men fully loaded. You can see why the legionary was
nick-named 'Marius' mule'.

Compare the equipment of 'Marius' mule' with that on pages 62 and 63. Although the details varied, a Roman legionary on the march carried much the same load for centuries after Marius. Though spades and baskets for shifting earth were packed with the tents and hand-mills on carts or baggage animals, each man carried a tool kit containing saw, axe, sickle, chain, rope. He had his own bronze dish and pan; some have been found with their owners' names. Food and spare clothes probably went into the string bag and sack.

Legions of men like these could march anywhere and beat any foe. They would follow a trusted general anywhere. When these men retired, they expected to be given a piece of land each, so as to be able to live as peasant farmers in the old-fashioned way. A good general tried to make sure that the Senate gave land to his old soldiers; if he did this, he could be sure that his men would be grateful and loyal to him.

Once a province had been conquered and was being protected by the legions, somebody had to govern it. Who? The Senate could think of nothing better than to send out a senator, often an ex-consul, for a year or two. Such a governor would have complete power over his province. He would often be a complete stranger to the place and to the job he had to do, and would only just be learning how to govern his province properly when the time came for him to go back to Rome. That meant that even the most honest men would probably not be able to do very well as governors of provinces.

Unfortunately, some of these governors were not honest men. Now that they had the chance, some of them made themselves very rich by forcing the people of the province to pay bribes and extra taxes, or even by simply robbing when they saw anything they wanted; even the temples of the gods were not safe against some of these bad governors. Some of the governors, and the friends they took out with them, came back to Rome fabulously rich.

Apart from any such blackmail and robbery, the people of the provinces had to pay taxes. The Romans thought that this was only fair. The Romans thought that they were bringing peace and civilization to the provinces, and that the provincial people should at least pay for what the Romans were giving them. Later in this book we shall see what benefits the Romans did bring to the people living in their Empire, but here we are concerned with the price that had to be paid.

The men who collected the taxes were called 'publicans'. You may have come across the word in the Bible, and you may have guessed what sort of a reputation publicans had. Some of them may have been honest, but it was thought that most of them took far more from the people of the province than they were supposed to, and put the surplus money into their own pockets.

These tax-collectors squeezed large sums of money out of the provinces, but much of that money was kept to make the publicans and their friends rich.

You may ask how they were able to do all this without being punished. In fact, some were punished – but they were the unlucky ones. It was the job of the governor of a province to control the publicans, and a good one would do so. A bad one, though, like the governors already described on this page, might prefer to work with the publicans, so that they could all get rich quicker together. There were too many rich Romans who had business reasons for not wanting to see things cleaned up. For Rome had changed. Though there was still plenty of talk about how a true Roman should behave, and though Romans often tried to live up to those ideals, there were too many Romans who had a new idea. This was that money was the only thing that counted; money could buy anything – and anybody.

In Rome –
richer rich and poorer poor

You know that there had been rich and poor in Rome for hundreds of years; you remember the trouble there had been between patricians and plebeians. Now the rich were becoming very rich indeed. You have just seen some of the ways in which some Romans made money. Others made money by becoming business men, merchants or money-lenders. Senators were not supposed to go in for things like that, but it was possible for them to buy clever slaves and set them up in business. By one method or another, a rich Roman could do very well indeed for himself.

Another way in which the rich became richer was by making big farms and using slaves to work on them. Rich Romans would buy lands that had been laid waste by war, or buy small farms from the peasants. There was nothing new in slavery, but huge estates worked entirely by slaves, while free Roman citizens were unable to find land to work for themselves – that was something new. The rich owners of these estates made money, while the poor Romans had to go to look for work in the cities.

What did the rich Romans do with all this money? They spent much of it on luxury, especially on enormous banquets of the most expensive food. Some of them even used to make themselves sick when they were full, so as to be able to go on eating. They could find nothing to do with all their wealth except amuse themselves, and even when they amused themselves they could think of nothing better than that.

Other rich Romans used their money in politics. They could bribe poor citizens to vote for them. They could hire gangsters and buy tough slaves to act as bodyguards, to beat up or to murder anyone who got in their way.

*the rich Roman lives
in a luxurious house*

*he gets wealth: from the provinc
from business, from his estates*

28

he has slaves:
to serve him,
to work for him,
to defend him

he has clients:
to vote for him
and make him important

so he can bully and bribe,
and live in luxury,
and do whatever he pleases

Meanwhile, what was happening to the poorer Romans? As you know, many of them were crowding into the city because they could no longer earn a living on the land. But here too there was so much cheap slave labour that free workmen found it hard to get jobs. Even when they did find work, the pay was low. It was a grim outlook for the poor Roman: a miserable life in a dirty jerry-built slum tenement, with a good chance of idleness and starvation. Was there anything that they could do about it? Would the poor Romans put up with this sort of thing, or would they rise against the rich Romans?

The rich Romans saw to it that the poor were not forced to do this. First, no free Roman need ever starve. The Roman government bought corn with the money which the provinces paid in taxes, and this corn was given as a free dole to the poorer citizens. Second, a poor Roman could become the client of a rich Roman. This meant that he could go every morning to greet his patron, as the rich man would be called, and the patron's slaves would hand out presents, money and food to the clients. In return for these presents, the clients had to vote the way their patron told them at elections, and generally hang about and make themselves useful to the patron.

So the poorer Romans would be kept alive. They would have bread. Would this be enough to prevent them from making trouble for the rich? There was something else; the poor had to be kept amused, to have something to look at and talk about. There were the public baths, where a man could lounge about all day in comfort. There were chariot races, spectacular, dangerous for the drivers, and exciting. Above all, there was the circus. This was where the biggest shows of all were held, where the Romans could sit safe and comfortable, watching hundreds of wild beasts, criminals, slaves and trained gladiators kill one another. If you remember what you read earlier in this book about the Romans, about what sort of people they had been, you may wonder that they could sink as low as this.

As a Roman writer said: 'Times change, and we change with the times.'

the poor Roman lives in a tenement

he has nothing

he is given: corn by the government,

presents by his patron,

so he can
hang about . . .
and amuse himself . . .
and do as his patron tells him

The republic goes rotten

CORRUPTION. You sometimes hear it said that politics are a dirty game. Certainly, like most games, politics can be played in a dirty way, especially by those people who just *must* win. You have learned enough about the rich and poor in Rome to know how citizens were bribed and how the Senate did not punish bad governors and publicans. Money had been used to make Rome corrupt. Worse was to come. The full story of the last hundred years of the Roman republic is complicated and nasty. Here are a few of the most famous facts; they will be enough to show you what was going on.

MURDER. Tiberius Gracchus was a tribune in 133 B.C. He tried to stop the rot by breaking up some of the big estates and giving land to the peasants. His enemies caused a riot in the Forum, and murdered him. Ten years later his brother Caius Gracchus became tribune and tried to do the same sort of thing. He also was murdered.

REVOLT OF THE ALLIES. Many of the Italian cities thought that the Romans were favouring themselves and enriching themselves, and they wanted equal shares. These people asked to be made Roman citizens. There was a fierce war, 91 to 88 B.C., which the Romans won. But the Romans were sensible enough to give citizenship to their allies, all the same, to prevent further trouble.

PRIVATE ARMIES. Marius was a successful general who became consul six times, and was very popular with his soldiers. When some of his enemies in Rome tried to prevent his ex-soldiers from being given land when they retired, Marius marched his troops into the Forum. His method of 'persuasion' worked. Afterwards, other generals copied his idea.

CIVIL WAR. Sulla was another successful general. He and his friends in the Senate disliked Marius and tried to keep him out of power. At last it came to fighting, the Roman legions of Marius against the Roman legions of Sulla.

MASSACRE. In 87 B.C. Marius took Rome; as he went through the streets, his men killed on the spot anyone Marius pointed out. A few years later, after Marius was dead, Sulla came back. He too slaughtered his enemies, but he was more careful than Marius. He had long lists of names prepared, and marked down those who were to be killed.

REVOLT OF THE SLAVES. Spartacus was a gladiator who escaped from his master in 73 B.C. and raised an army of escaped slaves. He defeated three Roman armies in southern Italy before he himself was defeated and killed in battle.

Wanted – a strong man

Rome was in a mess, and most of the Romans knew it. There was a lot of talk about 'the good old days', but nobody seemed to know how to bring back those days when the Romans had put Rome first and themselves second. The Senate and the consuls did not seem to be capable of doing their job properly.

When a state gets into a mess, people very often blame the government, because the government's job is to see that the state does not get into a mess. If things get no better, people sometimes wish that there were one strong man, a man who knows his own mind and who has the brains and the strength to rule the country properly. Sometimes there is a good supply of strong men who are perfectly willing to take over, just as the tyrants had done in the little Greek city-states. Now Rome was not a little city-state, but the mistress of a large Empire. Competition among would-be strong men was keen; and, knowing what you already know about Rome at this time, you will not need to be told that it was a contest with no holds barred.

Marius and Sulla had each been master of Rome in his time. When they died, there were others who tried either to lead the Senate or to overthrow it. The most famous and the most successful of these 'strong men' was Julius Caesar.

Julius Caesar was a very clever and very brave man who lived a life full of adventure. His life-story is well worth reading, but it needs a book to itself. Here we can do no more than look at what he managed to achieve. Of course, he began with the two great gifts we have just mentioned – brains and bravery. Without them he could have done very little.

There were two other advantages. He was born into one of the leading families in Rome, so he knew all the most important people. Also, he had money. He soon spent so much that he was badly in debt, but he was always able to borrow more; by the time he needed to borrow a lot of money, enough money-lenders thought that to lend to Caesar was like backing a winner.

One of the 'best' people.

Caesar won for himself two more advantages. He set out to make himself popular with the poorer Romans, and he succeeded. He knew how to win over crowds of the ordinary people and make them think that he was really fond of them. Then he got control of an army. He was given command of the legions in the south of Gaul, that is, the modern south of France. From 58 to 51 B.C. he led his army all over Gaul. He conquered the entire land and all its warrior tribes. He showed that he was a fine general, he trained his army well, and he won the loyalty of his legions so that they would follow him anywhere, against anybody.

Popular with the ordinary people.

By now the Senate saw the danger. There was a great war between Caesar and the Senate; the armies of the Senate were commanded by another great Roman general, Pompey, who had once been friendly with Caesar. Pompey was beaten in battle, fled to the kingdom of Egypt, and was murdered. Caesar became master of Rome and the whole of the Roman Empire in 46 B.C.

How would he use his power? Would he put an end to the corruption and disorder? Would he make the republic work properly once more? Perhaps he would have done the first, but it seemed certain that he would not do the second. In fact, it looked as though Caesar was not content only to have the power; he wanted the title of king also. There were still many

Julius Caesar. A portrait bust of the first century AD.

Caesar's dream

Romans who thought that people could not be free if they had a king. The word 'king' reminded a Roman of the old stories of the Tarquins, or made him think of the kings whom the Romans had fought and defeated in Africa and Asia. Some of the senators thought this, and decided to take the obvious way of preventing Caesar from making himself king. On 15 March (the Ides of March, as the day was called in the Roman calendar) in the year 44 B.C. Julius Caesar attended a meeting of the Senate. He had been warned that his life was in danger, but he took no notice of the warnings. The conspirators closed round him, and Caesar died with twenty-three dagger-thrusts in his body.

The reality

Antony, Cleopatra and Octavian

Mark Antony: an aureus minted in Rome, 39 BC.

Once more the struggle for power went on, the old dreary story of treachery, murder and civil war. One by one, the men who were fighting for power were knocked out of the contest. Most of them were killed, including Brutus and Cassius, who had led the conspiracy against Julius Caesar.

Eight years after Caesar's murder, the Roman Empire was shared between two very powerful men. One of them was Octavian, the great-nephew of Julius Caesar. Though he was not a particularly good general, he was very clever at politics, at persuading other people to do as he wanted. The other was Mark Antony, a famous general who had been at one time Julius Caesar's best friend, but who was often thoughtless and rash. Octavian stayed in Rome, and looked after the western part of the Roman Empire. Antony went to look after the eastern part, where there was a war against the Parthians, who were the strong new rulers of Persia. The picture map opposite will show you how Octavian and Antony worked.

Perhaps the two men would have quarrelled anyway, but it was Cleopatra, Queen of Egypt, who did in fact cause the quarrel. You may remember how, about 300 years before, Egypt had become a Hellenistic kingdom under one of the generals of Alexander the Great, and how the great city of Alexandria had become the most important Greek city in the Mediterranean. Cleopatra had no intention of letting her kingdom become part of the Roman Empire. Instead, she thought that she could use Antony and his legions to build up a new empire with its capital at Alexandria, not Rome. As everybody knows, Antony fell completely under the control of Cleopatra.

Many of Antony's old friends were disgusted, and many of the people of Rome were afraid that Antony and Cleopatra would do what Hannibal had failed to do. It was a fight between east and west, and Antony was a traitor. So Octavian now had a wonderful chance to rally all the Romans behind him. He did not waste the opportunity.

The battle which decided everything was a sea battle. The fleet of Antony and Cleopatra met the fleet of Octavian at Actium on 2 September, 31 B.C., and Octavian's men won a great victory. Antony and Cleopatra fled to Egypt, and when they realized that Octavian was bound to conquer and capture them, they committed suicide.

Cleopatra: a tetradrachm minted at Ascalon, 49 BC.

Rome

Actium

Alexandria

Fourteen years after Julius Caesar's death, his great-nephew was master of the Roman Empire, as Julius had been. Would Octavian be able to do any better than his great-uncle?

Augustus

Octavian is usually thought to have been the first Roman emperor. What was an emperor? The first thing to notice is that an emperor was *not* a king. The word that had cost Julius Caesar his life was never used about Octavian. To say what an emperor *was* is more difficult. The word 'emperor' is just another form of the Roman word 'imperator', and that simply means 'commander'. It was an unofficial title, almost a nickname, which the Roman legionaries would give to their general if he had done very well in a battle. Many Roman generals had been imperators, but from now onwards only one man at a time was entitled to the name. This is part of the secret. Octavian and the men who came after him knew that the first thing the ruler of Rome had to do was to make sure that he had command of the army, and to make sure that the army remained loyal by treating the soldiers well.

Hail Emperor!

But Octavian did not make the mistake of thinking that this was enough. He wanted his control over the army to be legal. He wanted the Senate to help him. So, instead of trying to weaken the Senate or even to get rid of it, he did the opposite. He went out of his way to be polite to the Senate and to see that senators were given dignified and well-paid jobs. Though, as everybody knew, he had the army behind him and could have done as he pleased, he took care only to do what would please the Senate and People of Rome. S.P.Q.R. were still the magic letters, and the Romans could say that Octavian was really just making the republic work properly once more.

Because Octavian was ready to make things easy for the Senate, the Senate was prepared to make things easy for Octavian. It was the same with the assembly of the Roman people in the Forum. So he, or one of his friends, was usually consul. He was given the powers and privileges of a tribune. He was, as you have seen, given the command of the army. It still sounded as if the republican system was working, because all these jobs had been well known for so long. But one man controlled all the really important jobs, and always got his own way. If this was a republic, it was a very queer one.

This map of the Empire will show you how Octavian worked. Some of the provinces were senatorial; that meant that the Senate appointed the governors, and these were very good jobs. But other provinces were imperial. Because these provinces were likely to cause trouble and need troops – you can see that they were mostly on the frontier, or newly conquered, or both – the imperator appointed the governors to them.

If Octavian had used his power badly, there still might have been trouble. But he ruled well. He trained and appointed reliable new civil servants to take the places of the old publicans, and sent out good governors to the provinces. He restored peace after years of war, and with peace came prosperity and justice. Octavian's friend, the great poet Virgil, wrote of how it was the destiny of Rome to beat down the proud in warfare, and to spare the defeated peoples within the Roman Empire. It was the duty of Rome to bring peace, prosperity and justice to all the peoples who lived around the Mediterranean Sea. This was the PAX ROMANA, the Roman Peace.

In the city of Rome itself, as well as in the rest of the Empire, Octavian cleaned things up in every way, including the buildings of the city. He himself boasted that he 'found Rome built of brick, and left it built of marble'.

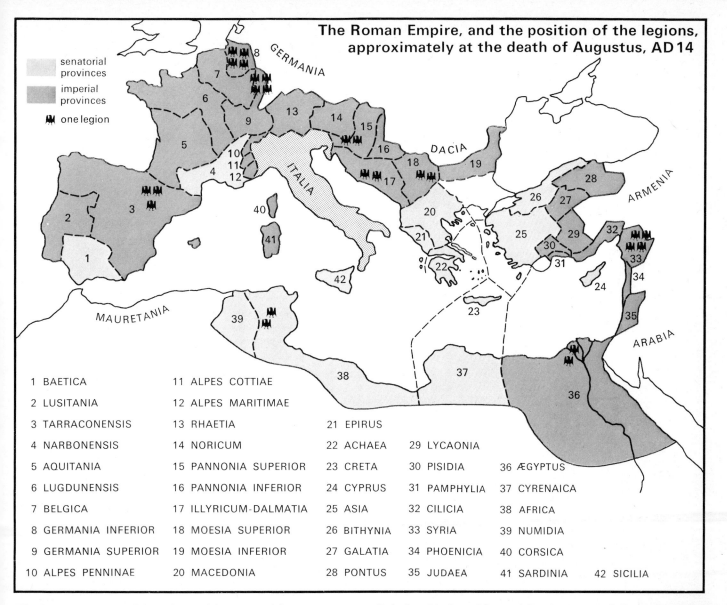

The Roman Empire, and the position of the legions, approximately at the death of Augustus, AD 14

senatorial provinces
imperial provinces
one legion

GERMANIA
ITALIA
DACIA
ARMENIA
MAURETANIA
ARABIA

1 BAETICA	11 ALPES COTTIAE			
2 LUSITANIA	12 ALPES MARITIMAE			
3 TARRACONENSIS	13 RHAETIA	21 EPIRUS		
4 NARBONENSIS	14 NORICUM	22 ACHAEA	29 LYCAONIA	
5 AQUITANIA	15 PANNONIA SUPERIOR	23 CRETA	30 PISIDIA	36 ÆGYPTUS
6 LUGDUNENSIS	16 PANNONIA INFERIOR	24 CYPRUS	31 PAMPHYLIA	37 CYRENAICA
7 BELGICA	17 ILLYRICUM-DALMATIA	25 ASIA	32 CILICIA	38 AFRICA
8 GERMANIA INFERIOR	18 MOESIA SUPERIOR	26 BITHYNIA	33 SYRIA	39 NUMIDIA
9 GERMANIA SUPERIOR	19 MOESIA INFERIOR	27 GALATIA	34 PHOENICIA	40 CORSICA
10 ALPES PENNINAE	20 MACEDONIA	28 PONTUS	35 JUDAEA	41 SARDINIA 42 SICILIA

The Senate was grateful, and gave him many titles.
He was called:

PRINCEPS, or First Citizen
PATER PATRIAE, or Father of the Fatherland
AUGUSTUS, or Worthy of Reverence.

It is by this last title, and by the name of Caesar, which he inherited from his great-uncle, that he is usually known. The emperors who followed him used both of those titles.

For, from this time onwards, the Roman Empire, though it still had consuls, tribunes, Senate and all the other republican names and officials, was to be ruled by an emperor.

left: Part of the ruins of the Roman Forum, where the people used to assemble during the republic.

right: A memorial statue to Augustus, showing him in full imperial dignity and authority.

LOOKING BACK

So far this book has been the story of one people – the Romans. We watched three things especially:

1. The qualities that the Romans claimed to have.
2. The way they governed themselves.
3. The growth of their Empire.

We saw that even if the famous stories of early Rome are probably no more than stories, the Romans really did have many outstanding qualities, which helped them to make their republic work well, and helped them to build up an Empire, first in Italy, then all over the Mediterranean.

Then we saw that possessing an Empire made so much difference to the Romans that the republic broke down.

So, finally, after many years of trouble, the Romans, their republic, and their Empire came to be ruled by emperors.

Now it is time for us to see what this great Roman Empire did for the people who belonged to it.

41

2. THE EMPIRE

Pax Romana

Augustus died in the year 14; not B.C., but A.D., for it was while he was ruling the Roman Empire that Jesus Christ was born. When Augustus died the Empire was about as big as it was going to be. These maps and graphs, which you can compare with the others on pages 18, 24 and 25, will show you the final stages in the growth of the Roman Empire.

It was a huge area to rule, and most of the emperors found that they had plenty to do in ruling it. There had to be some special reason for them to try to add any new provinces. Besides, if you look at the final map you will see other good reasons why the Empire should not grow any further – the sea, or waste lands, or enemies so strong that it was not worth while trying to beat them and then hold them down.

Look at a modern map, and find out how many modern countries are inside the frontiers of the old Roman Empire.

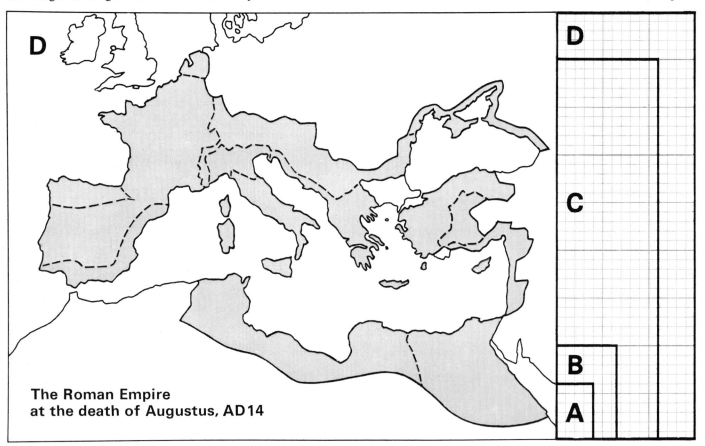

**The Roman Empire
at the death of Augustus, AD 14**

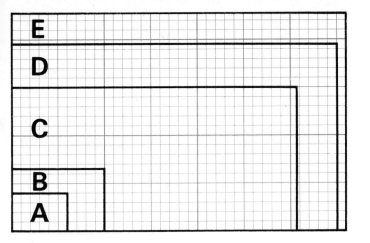

The roads

Everybody knows that the Romans were great road-builders. Most have heard the saying: 'All roads lead to Rome.' If you put these two bits of information together, you may guess the main reason for those fine roads – to keep Rome in touch with her Empire. Those roads were like the nerves in a human body, sending messages and receiving instructions; Rome was the brain. The roads were also like the arteries of a body, carrying life and strength; Rome was the heart. Along the roads of the Empire sped the chariots of the imperial messengers, from post-house to post-house, and along the roads swung the legions and the auxiliaries, eating up the distances with their measured, unhurried steps. The roads held the Empire together.

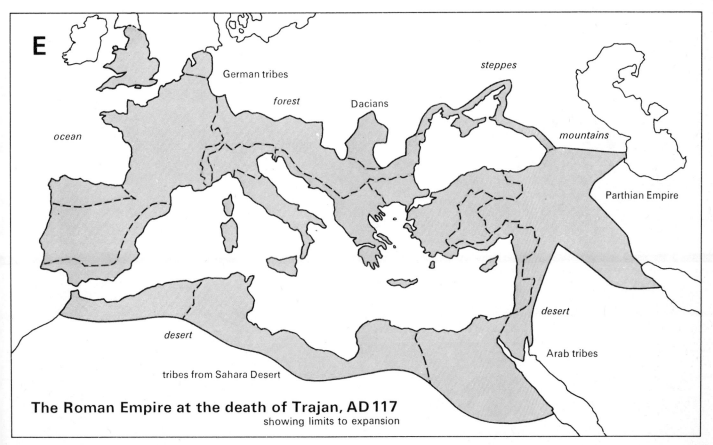

The Roman Empire at the death of Trajan, AD 117
showing limits to expansion

As you can see from the picture, the roads were built with very great skill and care. As you can see from the map, the main roads linked all parts of the Empire together, and there were great towns or fortresses where the roads joined. Some of these cities were older than Rome itself, but many were founded by the Romans. Once again you may find it interesting to compare the map with a modern atlas; see how many modern roads and railways follow the routes of the Romans, and how many great modern cities owe their positions and sometimes their names to the Romans. Some of these roads and some of these cities were built where, before the Romans came, there had been only wilderness, rough and often dangerous tracks, and the crude villages of fierce tribes.

Now there was peace and safety. Merchants could travel freely, without an armed escort, from one end of the Empire to another. Farms and towns could prosper, and, in the towns especially, people could enjoy the comforts of Roman civilization, thanks to the skill of Roman engineers.

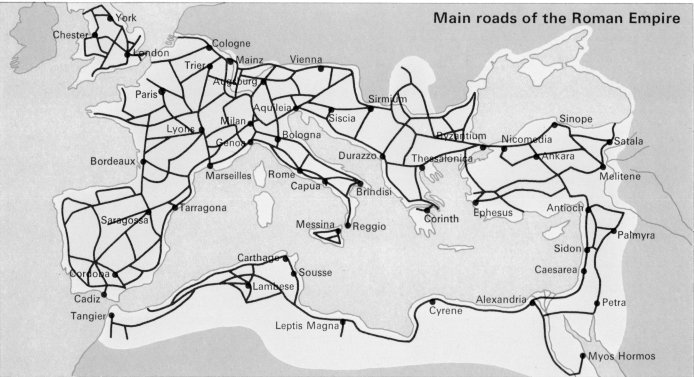

Main roads of the Roman Empire

The buildings

When Mount Vesuvius erupted in A.D. 79 the town of Pompeii was in a few hours smothered under a huge layer of ashes. There it lay, preserved like a mummy, until in modern times the ashes were removed. Ostia was a bustling sea-port which decayed, was deserted, fell slowly into ruins. It has now been restored by archaeologists so well that, as in Pompeii, visitors can walk along the streets, enter the shops and houses, and imagine what life was like in an Italian town at the height of the Roman Empire.

From that buried town we can get our most vivid pictures of Roman life, but in many places, in all parts of what was the Roman Empire, there are still great buildings standing. In Spain, for instance, if you come to the famous university city of Salamanca from the south, you will cross the River Tormes on a Roman bridge. In another Spanish city, Segovia, there is a magnificent aqueduct–a sort of bridge to carry a channel for water to run to the city. The aqueduct of Segovia was still doing its job, bringing water to the people of the town, until a few years ago.

above: Roman bridge at Salamanca.

left: Roman aqueduct at Segovia.

left: Porta Nigra, Trier, built in the late third or early fourth century AD.

right: Colosseum, built in the late first century AD.

Around these towns would be walls, more to keep out beasts and criminals and to make it easy for the town councils to control traffic than because of serious danger of warfare. This great gate at Trier, in Western Germany, is obviously meant to look grand and impressive rather than to be used in fighting. The corner tower of the walls of York is more business-like, but then York was a legionary base, and not far from the frontier. (Only the bottom of the tower is Roman; the walls went on being used for a thousand years and more, and the top had to be rebuilt during the Middle Ages.)

The great public buildings, so strongly built that their solidity amazes tourists, can still be seen in many towns, especially in France and Italy. Here are a few of the most famous. In Rome itself there is the gigantic arena, the Colosseum, with its rows of seats supported on rows of arches. Just as famous is the temple of the Pantheon, with its great arched circular roof, or dome. If you look at these pictures of Roman buildings, you will notice how much the Roman engineers used this idea of the arch. Sometimes the Romans would build a fine arch as a monument, often to a victory. This shows you the triumphal arch in the town of Orange, in the south of France.

It would be easy to go on filling page after page with pictures of the splendid work of Roman architects and engineers, for it was in practical things like this that the Romans were specially good. They were not such great artists as the Greeks, but they were great engineers.

left: Multangular tower at York; the lower part, dating from about AD 300, is Roman.

right: Pantheon, first quarter of the second century AD.

far right: Arch at Orange commemorating a victory over the Gauls in the first century BC, though possibly built later.

An imperial palace

One very striking example may sum up the size and strength with which the Romans could build. Over 1,600 years ago the Emperor Diocletian built himself a palace beside the Adriatic Sea, in the country we know today as Yugoslavia. *Inside* that

palace there grew up the entire city of Split. These two pictures, a photograph of modern Split and a reconstruction drawing of how the palace must have looked when it was built, will show you how the Roman palace has lived on in the modern town. The cathedral, the walls and gates, even the street plan and the walls of many of the houses are the work of the old Roman engineers.

Ostia was the seaport of Rome, at the mouth of the Tiber. Much of the town has been excavated and partly restored. Here are photographs of a street, and of a reconstruction model of a block of flats. The people who lived in them would be ordinary town-dwellers, not rich but not poor either.

In Pompeii there were many houses belonging to people with money to spend on comfort and elegance. This is the central courtyard of one such house.

Writing materials are among the small objects found in houses all over the Roman Empire; this group comes from London. There are pens of the stylus type, with a sharp point for writing on wax-coated tablets, and a flat end for rubbing out. Another pen has a spoon at the end, for mixing ink. One of the inkpots is for a desk, but the other could be carried. The small metal box was fitted over the knot of string round a parcel, to protect the seal.

A street in Pompeii.

There were paintings on the walls of many Roman houses. This is one of the large number found in southern Italy, and shows a young woman using a stylus and tablets.

Justice . . .

The Romans made laws the way they made buildings. They were good engineering jobs, they worked and they were sound enough to go on working for a long time.

This was their problem. Inside the Empire there were all sorts of people, of all races, colours, languages, religions, customs and laws. There were forest-dwellers and desert-dwellers, farmers and townsmen of all sorts. There were Italians, Gauls, Spaniards, Germans, Moors, Britons, Syrians, Greeks, Egypt-ians, Dalmatians, Arabs – and more and more peoples. Yet they all had to live together in peace. That meant that they all had to obey one law. If you remember Hammurabi, you will remember how important that was.

The Roman lawyers solved the problem by working out codes (sets) of laws which were so fair and so clear that all the different nations in the Empire could see that they were good. A Greek and a Gaul might have had different customs at home, for example, but if they were both to meet while trading in Sicily and were to have a quarrel, the Roman judges would be able to decide the case by looking up a big code of laws which covered all of the people in the Empire. Just as modern philosophers still study Greek philosophy because of what it can teach them, modern lawyers in many countries still study Roman law.

Marcus Aurelius, last of the 'Five Good Emperors',
shared his duties and powers with a co-emperor,
Lucius Verus, shown on this coin.

. . . for all

This law and this justice were for everybody in the Empire. They were not only for Romans, not only for the people of one or two provinces. It is true that the Roman citizen had certain privileges; for instance, if he was not satisfied with the verdict of a judge, he could appeal to the emperor in Rome. You may remember from the Bible how St Paul was sent to Rome when he appealed to Caesar.

St Paul could do this because he was a Roman citizen. Yet he was a Jew from Asia. How could such a man be a Roman? The answer is that anyone who seemed loyal to Rome could become a Roman citizen, no matter what he had been born. It was a privilege open to anyone who earned it. Soldiers who had served their full time in auxiliary regiments became citizens when they retired from the army. Even slaves were made citizens when they were given their freedom.

At last, in 212, Emperor Caracalla made all the free men who lived in the Empire Roman citizens. The city had grown into an Empire where all free men were equal in law.

With this idea of treating people fairly, according to the law, there was sometimes another: the idea of trying to pick the best man for any important job. Some of the emperors tried to do this by using loyal and intelligent ex-slaves, or freedmen, to help them to run the Empire. Some emperors carefully selected young men who seemed to be wise and strong, and adopted them so that they would become the next emperors. Partly because of this, there was a line of very good emperors, 'the Five Good Emperors', between 96 and 180. With men like these ruling wisely and enforcing the Roman law, the Empire was a place where most men could peacefully earn their living, safe from war and from unfair treatment.

Tolerance . . .

The Romans had always been people more interested in practical things than in arguing about religion and the gods. The peoples who were brought into the Empire usually had their own gods, and wanted to go on worshipping them. This did not worry the Romans. Roman soldiers seem to have picked up the habit of worshipping all sorts of strange gods, according to where they were stationed. For instance, a soldier might find that the local people had never heard of Mars, but had their own war-god who was called Thincsus. So he would say, 'Your Thincsus seems to be the same god as our Mars. We are really all worshipping the same god.' Sometimes an altar would be set up with both names on it, and so everybody would be content. The Romans were ready to allow people to worship whatever gods they wished, as long as this worship did not interfere with loyalty to Rome. They were tolerant about religion; that means they did not believe in quarrelling over it.

. . . for most

Does that statement about Roman tolerance make sense to you? What about all those Christians and lions in the arena?

The trouble was that the Christians seemed not to be loyal. The Romans decided that it would be a good idea to treat their emperor as a god, with temples and altars. It would be an easy way of giving everybody in the Empire a way of showing loyalty. It was just a matter of dropping a few grains of incense or a little wine in the hollow on top of the altar. But Christians refused to do anything like this: they would worship only one God. The Romans could not understand the Christian idea, and thought that a God who would not allow full respect to be shown to the Emperor must be a very dangerous God. They felt that Christians could easily be traitors to Rome.

The Jews, too, felt the wrath of Rome—and the Christian religion was at first very much tied up with the Jews. The Jews rose twice against the Romans, and put up such a fierce fight in their stronghold of Jerusalem that at last the Romans decided that the only way of preserving peace in future was to drive all the Jews out of Palestine. The exile of the Jews was to last 1,800

far left: This pillar was part of a shrine to Mars Thincsus, built by German soldiers stationed at Housesteads.

left: Altar dedicated by men of Legion VI Victrix (Victorious) to the supreme god, Jupiter Dolichenus the Eternal, and to the local gods of the Brigantian district.

years, and their return to Palestine has produced one of the most difficult political problems of our own century. In this way the power of Rome has reached across the centuries.

But Christians, Jews, and also the Druids of Britain, were exceptions. Usually the Romans were willing to welcome any new god, such as the Persian Mithras, who did not seem to be an enemy of the Emperor.

Part of a mosaic of the fourth century AD. The gladiators' names are given. If he lived long enough a gladiator might become a 'star', idolized by his 'fans'.

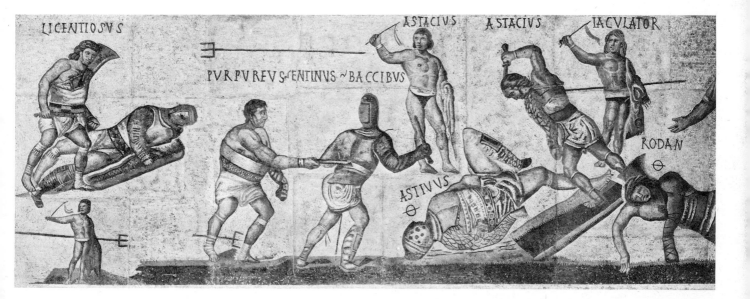

The price

We have been looking at the good side of the Roman Empire. Do not forget that there was a bad side, too. In Rome itself 'Bread and Circuses' still went on; the cruel shows in the arena were probably bigger and worse than they had been in the days of the republic. The people had peace and justice and enough to eat, and they had their amusements. But that was all. Can you think of anything that was missing? Anything that they did not have?

Only the emperor and his servants had any real power. That was part of the price which the people of Rome and the Empire paid for the peace and law and order.

Another part of the price was paid in money. The taxes were not light.

Was the price a fair one? Did the people of the Roman Empire get good value for what they had given? It is a very difficult question to answer, and we ought to know far more about the details of life in the Roman Empire before we make up our minds. Yet it is an important question, one worth thinking about. Many things have changed between Roman times and our own, but sooner or later most of us have to answer for ourselves this question: what do we really want, and what are we prepared to pay for it?

Since we do not hear much about revolts or riots, it seems that, on the whole, the people of the Roman Empire probably thought that they were not paying too much for all that they got from Pax Romana, the Roman Peace.

The Roman conquest of Britain

In the year 43 Emperor Claudius sent an army to Britain. He was going to make the southern part of Britain, at least, a province of the Roman Empire.

Why had the emperor decided to do this? One reason was that some British princes who had quarrelled with their tribes and had been driven out of Britain asked for Roman help in getting back. This, though, was not a very good reason for sending such a big army; the emperor was not doing this to please one or two British princes. A better reason was that Britain was very near Gaul, and the tribes of Britain sometimes helped any Gauls who still tried to make trouble for the Romans. That was why Julius Caesar, a hundred years before in 55 and 54 B.C., had raided Britain and taught the most powerful tribes a lesson; but the lesson had not turned out to be good enough, and plans had later been made by Augustus to conquer Britain, though he was always too busy to put his plans into action. Now Claudius had the time, and he also wanted to win a victory somewhere, to make his people admire and respect him more. Claudius himself was a peaceful man, but he knew that people would respect him more if they thought that he was good at fighting.

There was always the chance, of course, that Britain would turn out to be rich enough to be worth having. There was some good land for growing corn, and there were some useful minerals – lead, tin, a little silver and gold. But on the whole Britain had the reputation of being an unattractive place, very misty and damp.

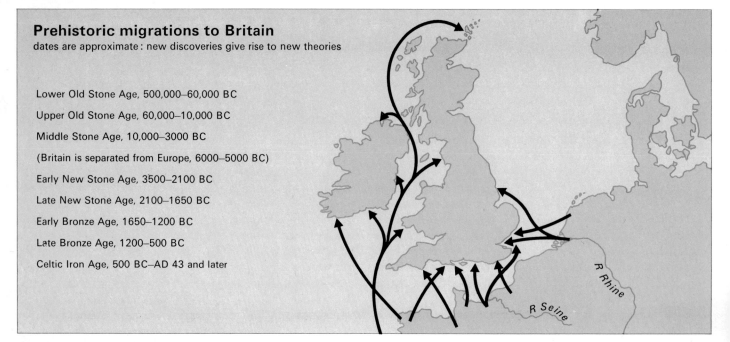

Prehistoric migrations to Britain
dates are approximate: new discoveries give rise to new theories

Lower Old Stone Age, 500,000–60,000 BC

Upper Old Stone Age, 60,000–10,000 BC

Middle Stone Age, 10,000–3000 BC

(Britain is separated from Europe, 6000–5000 BC)

Early New Stone Age, 3500–2100 BC

Late New Stone Age, 2100–1650 BC

Early Bronze Age, 1650–1200 BC

Late Bronze Age, 1200–500 BC

Celtic Iron Age, 500 BC–AD 43 and later

R Rhine

R Seine

Britain before the Romans came

The Romans were not the first people to invade Britain. During the thousands of years of prehistory there had been wave after wave of invasion. Sometimes, as far as we can tell, the invaders had come in peace, for there was plenty of room in Britain. At other times, the new people seem to have been well-armed and warlike.

If you look at any map of Europe, or even of the world, you will see that tribes of prehistoric men could move, or be pushed by stronger tribes, from the middle of the great land mass of Europe and Asia until they reached Britain. It was not too difficult to sail across the Channel. Archaeologists have been able to work out the routes by which many of these peoples moved to Britain by digging up their graves and looking at the things buried with their dead, and the map opposite will show you some of the different peoples and the directions in which they migrated.

You will notice that after the Old Stone Age people there came, first, the New Stone Age farmers. Then came peoples who knew about tools and weapons made of bronze. Then came tribes, one after another, who had iron as well. Each new people was probably a little stronger in war than the people before, and this may have meant that the earlier peoples were pushed into the north and west while the stronger tribes with the best tools and weapons lived in the south and east.

You do not need to know much geography to know that the north and west of Britain are more rocky, rainy and cold than the other parts, and that therefore they are not so good as the other parts for most sorts of farming. The bird's-eye picture below shows you that about 2,000 years ago the land in the south and east was very divided, too. You can see from this how the low hills of chalk and limestone ran across the country, and how between them lay the river valleys with forests and swamps. Most of the prehistoric peoples had preferred the hills, where it was so much easier to move about, to keep flocks and herds, and to farm without having to cut down lots of big trees or to drain marshy land. That is why by far the greatest number of important remains of prehistoric peoples in Britain have been found on these hills – New Stone Age burial mounds, or barrows; Bronze Age temples; Iron Age hill-forts.

Belas Knap, Gloucestershire. A New Stone Age barrow, over 60 yards (55 m) long. The 'front entrance' is a dummy, perhaps intended to deceive evil spirits. Thirty bodies were found in burial chambers within the mound.

Avebury Ring, Wiltshire. The largest of the henges, or sacred enclosures, built by New Stone Age and Bronze Age peoples. Many stones have been removed, but the plan still shows clearly. By the road in the top left corner are two parallel lines of stones, part of an avenue leading to another henge over a mile away.

Maiden Castle, Dorset. One of the largest Iron Age hill forts, enclosing 45 acres (18 hectares). It was skilfully designed with multiple ramparts, and an elaborately defended entrance at each end.

By the time the Romans came, there were farms like this in the southern part of Britain. The picture below shows a reconstruction of a farm which archaeologists discovered at Little Woodbury on Salisbury Plain. You can see how a British farmer 2,000 years ago would live with his family, slaves and animals. If danger threatened, they would all probably take shelter in the hill-fort of the local chief.

Coins from pre-Roman, first-century-AD Britain. A gold stater of Cunobelin, minted at Colchester; a silver coin of Cunobelin's brother, Epaticcus, showing the head of Hercules; a stater of the Coritani tribe, the letters VM probably forming part of a chieftain's name.

These Britons were not primitive savages, and they were not living in the Old Stone Age. They were capable of making such beautiful bronze-work as you can see on the opposite page; they obviously had superb artists and craftsmen, and there were chiefs who loved to have such things. These all cost something, but we know that the tribes of southern Britain had traders and had money. Here are some of their coins.

The next map shows you where the different tribes lived. Look especially at one tribe in the south-east, a tribe called the Catuvellauni. They were one of a group of tribes called Belgae, who had started to come to Britain from northern Gaul about 100 B.C. The Catuvellauni were very strong and aggressive. Under their king Cunobelin they had already conquered some of their neighbours, and looked like going on to conquer more. From his own capital at Verulamium and from the capital of the conquered Trinovantes at Camulodunum, King Cunobelin exercised power. These places were very rough towns, probably more like a sprawling clump of huts and wooden farm-houses; but they were more than farms and more than villages, and their ruler was the most important man in southern Britain.

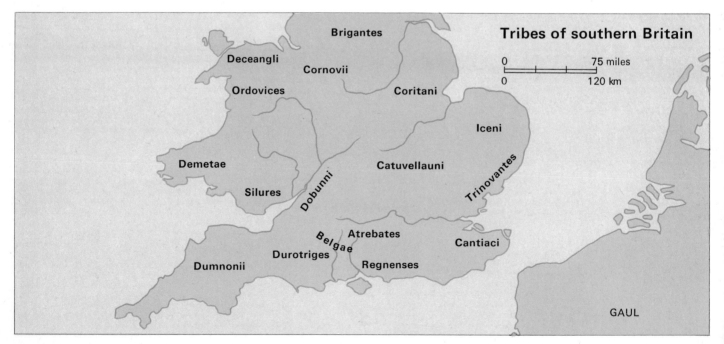

Tribes of southern Britain

0 ————————————— 75 miles
0 ————————————— 120 km

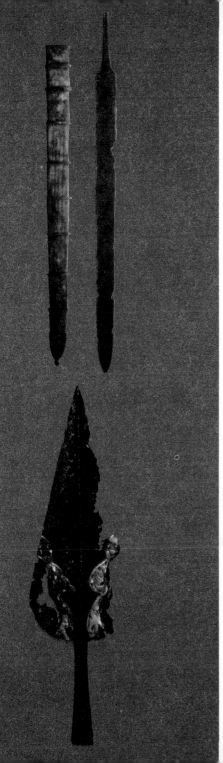

British arms about the time of the Roman invasion

Swords were long, meant to be swung in cutting, smashing blows. This one is 40 inches (1 m) long, of iron; its scabbard is of bronze-bound ash wood. It was found in a ditch of the Brigantian fort at Stanwick, Yorkshire.

The shield, found in the Thames at Battersea, is 32 inches (81 cm) long, made of gilt bronze. There is red glass in the ornamental studs. Spears and javelins were common weapons. The spearhead of iron had bronze decoration.

The bronze helmet has a neckguard like those on Roman helmets, but the curving decoration is typical of the Celtic style. There may have been cheek-pieces, and there was certainly a crest on top.

Cunobelin had died only a year or two before the Roman invasion, but he had left behind two sons, Caratacus and Togodumnus, who were carrying on where he had left off. These two princes gathered together the strong Catuvellaunian army, skilled warriors with iron spears and swords, with armour and shields of leather and bronze, and the swift, deadly chariots. It was this force, and not a gang of blue-painted savages waving stone clubs (as many people seem to think), which met the legions.

The Roman army

The Britons were bold warriors, but the Romans were well-trained soldiers. Look at the pictures opposite. See how well designed the legionary's clothing and armour are, so as to protect the vital parts of his head and body without interfering with his freedom to move. See how well designed his shield is to protect him, to fit together with the shields of his friends to form a solid wall or 'tortoise' covering over their heads; not to mention the edges and the centre-boss, which could give a hard knock to an enemy who rushed in too close.

Each man had a pair of javelins. Imagine what it must have been like when hundreds of soldiers hurled them at the same moment. These javelins were specially designed so that if they stuck in an enemy's shield they would bend or break when they were being pulled out, and so they could not be hurled back at the Romans. After the volleys of javelins, the Romans relied on the sword, not the long slashing sword of barbarians like the Britons, but the short thrusting sword which was quicker and gave more dangerous wounds.

Now think about all the people who helped the legions; there were engineers to plan camps and forts, doctors to cure the wounded, light troops on horses, or with slings or bows, artillerymen with their catapults. All these were there to support the legionary. Even without them, the legionary was capable of carrying all he needed. Look at the picture on page 26. Stakes, spades, hatchets, baskets, pots and pans and the food to go in them; quite apart from his arms and armour, the legionary carried equipment which weighed over forty pounds.

Roman arms about the time of the conquest of Britain

right: The replica Roman equipment shows how a legionary would appear in battle. The helmet is one of the best-known types, and the body-armour is one version of the 'waistcoat' of sliding iron strips which was the commonest legionary armour for a long time.

below: A slightly different version of the 'waistcoat', opened to show how it was constructed and how it could be put on.

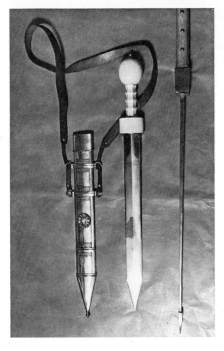

A closer view of the reconstructed javelin and sword. Legionary javelins were about 7 feet (2·1 m) long, swords about 2 feet (60 cm).

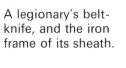

A legionary's belt-knife, and the iron frame of its sheath.

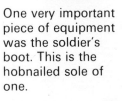

One very important piece of equipment was the soldier's boot. This is the hobnailed sole of one.

The Roman army was trained to fight almost like a machine. When marching into enemy country, the men would halt early in the afternoon; then half would pitch tents and dig ditches and throw up earth ramparts round the camp, while the other half stood guard. Every man knew what jobs had to be done, and how to do them. It was the same in battle. Every man knew how important it was to keep his place in the line, with exactly the right amount of space to use his weapons, and how important it was to obey orders. Compared with the planned, disciplined movements of the Romans, the British warriors seemed partly a mob, partly every-man-for-himself. Finally, when they had won, the Roman soldiers lost no time in building forts to watch the new frontier and roads to join the forts together.

That was the manner in which the legions of Emperor Claudius advanced into Britain.

The advance of the legions

These maps, especially if you have a good physical map of Britain beside them, will show you the main stages in the Roman conquest.

The first map shows you how the Romans landed, beat the army of Caratacus and Togodumnus, and pushed on to the Thames. They had to find a good crossing of this river before they could go any further north, and they picked on a place where they could ford, build a bridge, and bring ships easily. That place they called Londinium: you know its modern name. The Catuvellauni gave in, and the other tribes of the south-east seem to have been quite happy to have the Romans instead of the Catuvellauni. So the Romans pushed on, without much real fighting except in the west, until they reached that limestone ridge we saw in the bird's-eye picture on page 57. This seems to have been their frontier, and perhaps they did not intend to take any more of Britain.

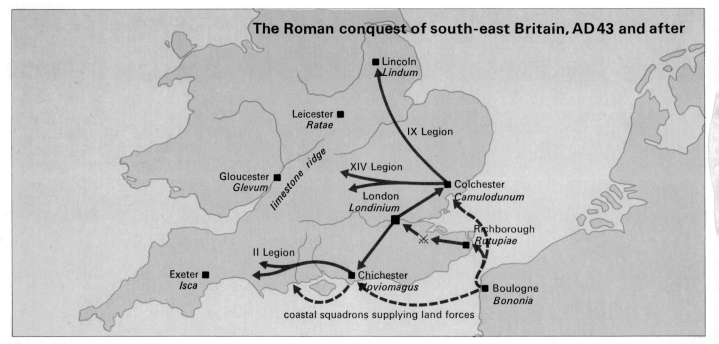

The Roman conquest of south-east Britain, AD 43 and after

coastal squadrons supplying land forces

The second map shows what happened. Caratacus had escaped west, and stirred up the tribes there to attack the Romans. At last he was beaten and betrayed to the Romans, in 51, but the trouble with the tribes in Wales went on. The Romans thought that the Druid priests were at the bottom of it, and attacked the Druid stronghold of Anglesey and massacred the Druids, in 60.

Meanwhile a great danger suddenly flared up in the southeast. Some of the Roman officials and some of the ex-soldiers who had been given lands and founded a colony at Camulodunum had treated the local British tribes very badly. There was a revolt, led by the widow Queen of the Iceni, Boudicca. Thousands of Romans and Britons who had sided with them were killed, often very cruelly. Camulodunum, Londinium and Verulamium were destroyed. The Ninth Legion was overcome by enormous numbers of the rebels, and almost wiped out. It looked for a while as though the Roman army in north Wales was cut off, doomed. But that army turned back and met the enormous hordes of Boudicca. Roman discipline and training defeated British fury and numbers. Boudicca committed suicide, and at first the Roman soldiers took a terrible revenge on the Britons. Soon, though, the government in Rome realized that the revolt of Boudicca had been mostly caused by the bad behaviour of the Romans themselves, so it ordered that the punishments should be stopped and took care that in future better officials were sent to rule the Britons.

One of the best Roman governors was Agricola, who ruled Britain between 78 and 85. He decided that the Romans had now gone so far that the only wise thing to do was to finish the job by conquering the whole of Britain. First he advanced on both sides of the Pennines, defeating the powerful tribe of the Brigantes, who had previously shown that they did not like the Romans. He built forts and roads to help him to keep the Brigantes quiet when he was further north, and then he went on to conquer Caledonia. (We call that country Scotland today, but in those days all the Scottish tribes were living in Ireland; so it is less confusing if we stick to the Roman name.) He beat the Caledonian tribes in the great battle of Mons Graupius, and was going to finish off Caledonia and then conquer Hibernia (which we nowadays call Ireland) when the emperor called him back to Rome.

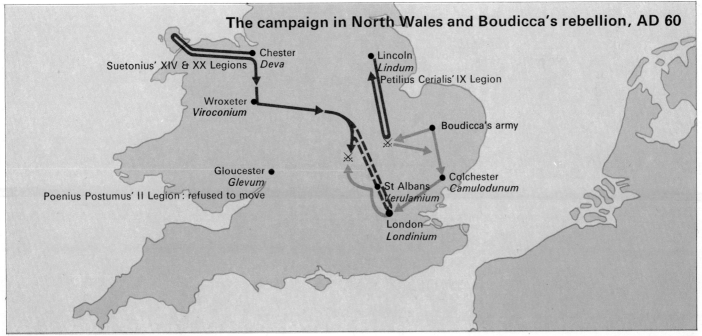

The campaign in North Wales and Boudicca's rebellion, AD 60

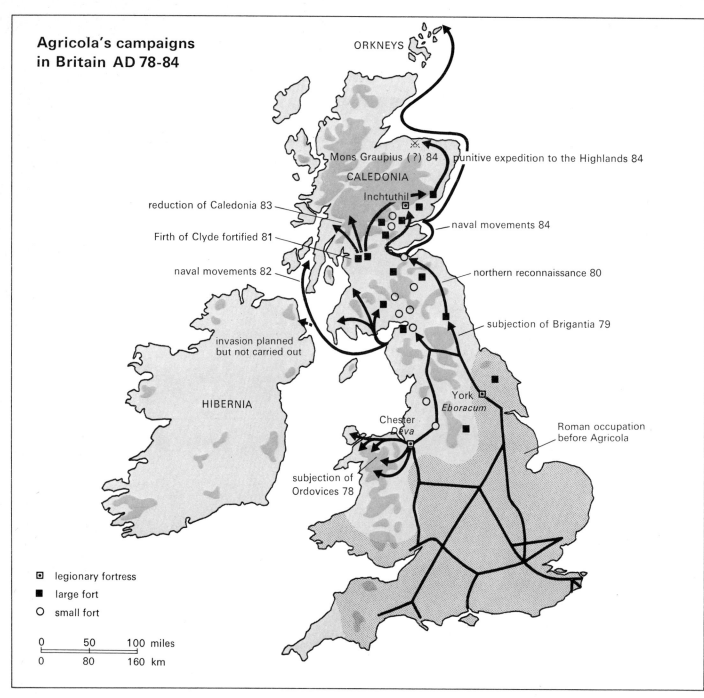

Agricola's campaigns in Britain AD 78-84

ORKNEYS

Mons Graupius (?) 84   punitive expedition to the Highlands 84

CALEDONIA

Inchtuthil

reduction of Caledonia 83

naval movements 84

Firth of Clyde fortified 81

naval movements 82

northern reconnaissance 80

subjection of Brigantia 79

invasion planned
but not carried out

HIBERNIA

York
Eboracum

Chester
Deva

Roman occupation
before Agricola

subjection of
Ordovices 78

◉ legionary fortress

■ large fort

○ small fort

| 0 | 50 | 100 miles |
| 0 | 80 | 160 km |

Far beyond the Roman frontier, in present-day Scotland, by the northern seas: the people lived in clusters of low stone huts, or sometimes in high round towers with galleries in the thickness of the walls.
above: The Jarlshof settlement in the Shetlands.
above left: This broch — as the towers are called — is only a few miles away, at Mousa.

The Roman conquest was over. It seems that in Rome the government of the emperor thought that it was a mistake to add Caledonia and Hibernia to the Empire. If the Roman government thought that those lands were too wild and poor to be worth the trouble and expense of ruling, they may have been right. But by stopping the conquest of Britain like that, the Romans gave themselves trouble and expense in another way. Now they had to make a frontier and defend it.

Roman marching camps at Pennymuir, Roxburghshire. They may have been made not in war but as training exercises.

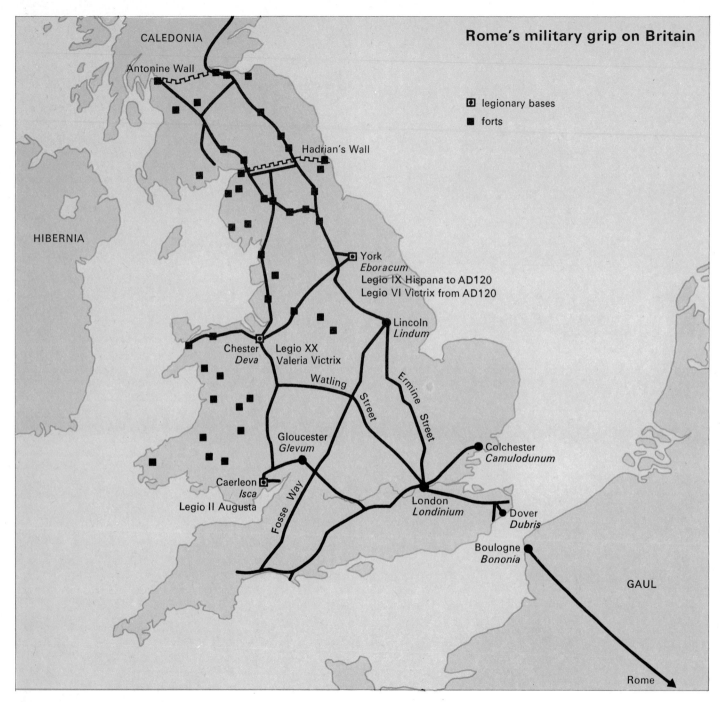

Rome's military grip on Britain

CALEDONIA

Antonine Wall

Hadrian's Wall

HIBERNIA

York
Eboracum
Legio IX Hispana to AD120
Legio VI Victrix from AD120

Lincoln
Lindum

Chester
Deva
Legio XX
Valeria Victrix

Watling

Ermine Street

Street

Gloucester
Glevum

Colchester
Camulodunum

Caerleon
Isca
Legio II Augusta

Fosse Way

London
Londinium

Dover
Dubris

Boulogne
Bononia

GAUL

Rome

☑ legionary bases
■ forts

Roman defence of Britain

If the Romans were going to have any more trouble in Britain, it would probably be in the north and the west. You can easily see why. In Wales lived the fierce tribes who had taken so much conquering, and who would probably rise against the Romans if they got the chance. The mountainous country would make it easy for rebels and outlaws. Besides, Hibernia lay across the sea, not too far away for raiders and pirates. So the Romans would have to see that plenty of soldiers were ready in the west.

The north was more dangerous still. The Brigantes were still enemies, even though they had been conquered, and further north were all the wild tribes of Caledonia. They would soon forget how they had been beaten by Agricola.

This map shows you how the Romans guarded against those dangers. All over the north and Wales there were forts for auxiliary soldiers. There would perhaps be about 500 men in each fort, and they would patrol the country around, watching for any signs of a revolt or a raid. These forts were linked, of course, by roads. The auxiliary troops would be able to do all the ordinary work; they were as much policemen as soldiers.

If really serious trouble broke out, if a big force of Caledonians, for example, came and joined up with Brigantian rebels, that would be too much for the auxiliaries. That would be work for the legions. You can see from the map how well the Romans placed their three legions in Britain, so that there were two ready to close in on the north and two ready to close in on the west. (It was not very likely that there would be really serious fighting in both the north and Wales at the same time.)

Then there was the question of reinforcements and supplies. You can see the great main roads spreading out from Londinium, with another main road running across from southwest to north-east. South from London the road went to Dubris, where there still stands part of a Roman lighthouse; and across the Channel lay the rest of the Roman Empire.

The Roman lighthouse at Dover today, and as it may have been in Roman times.

Finally, there were the ships. There was a small fleet to patrol the seas around Britain. Though its main port was on the south side of the Channel, at Bononia (Boulogne is the modern name), this fleet was called the British Fleet.

You can see that all this is very sensible. It should have worked, and on the whole it seems to have worked well. One or two improvements had to be made, though. The first was in the north.

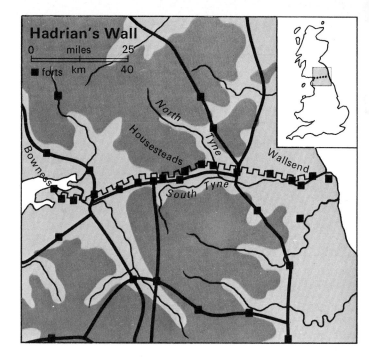

Hadrian's Wall

0   miles   25
■ forts   km   40

North Tyne
Housesteads
South Tyne
Bowness
Wallsend

Hadrian's Wall

The shorter a frontier is, the easier it is to watch and defend. So a glance at the map should be enough to show you why the Romans made their frontier between the Tyne and the Solway. When the Emperor Hadrian visited Britain in 121 there had been some sort of serious trouble, though we do not know the details. It may even have been so bad that the Ninth Legion, stationed at Eboracum (York), had disgraced itself and been disbanded; this is one of the puzzles of Romano-British history. Hadrian had decided anyway that the Empire was quite big enough, and that his best plan was to make frontiers which could be protected very easily. He did in Britain as he did in other parts of the Empire, built a wall along the frontier.

These sketches will show you that the wall was built in a strong position, as well as being made as short as possible. From the top of the wall, and from the look-out towers which were built every third of a mile, the sentries could easily see what was going on to the north, and send signals. But raiders could not see what was going on behind the wall.

The wall itself was about fifteen feet high, and there would have been a parapet about six feet high on top of that. In front

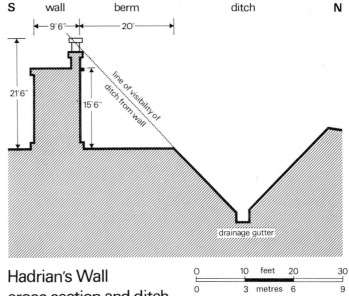

Hadrian's Wall
cross section and ditch

The north bank, built up with earth from the ditch, was sloped to give the sentry a clear view.

A model mile-castle
with its barracks,
storerooms, road
running through,
and watch-tower over
the north gate.

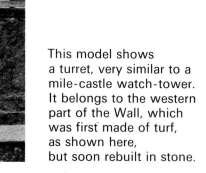

This model shows
a turret, very similar to a
mile-castle watch-tower.
It belongs to the western
part of the Wall, which
was first made of turf,
as shown here,
but soon rebuilt in stone.

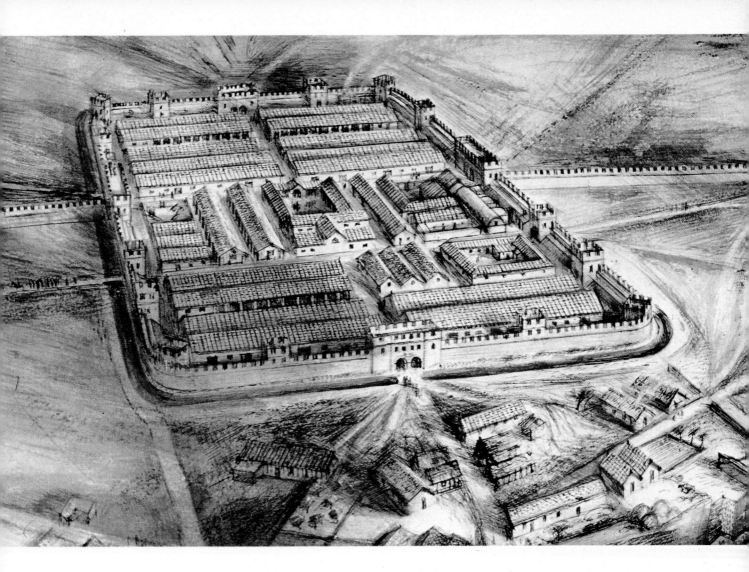

Chesters Fort, Northumberland, as it probably looked when the Second Ala of Asturian cavalry lived there. Three of the main gates were north of the Wall.

was a ditch, except where the ground dropped away so steeply that it was not needed. Every Roman mile (1,620 yards) there was a very small fort, holding about twenty or thirty auxiliary soldiers. These little forts are nowadays called mile-castles, because we do not know what the Romans called them. Between each pair of mile-castles the Romans built two watch-towers or turrets, where a few sentries could shelter. These men would be able to see that smugglers or robbers could not easily get into or out of the Roman part of Britain. Any Caledonians who

The most famous of all views of Hadrian's Wall. It is near Housesteads.

tried to steal cattle, for instance, from the farms on the Roman side of the wall would find it very difficult indeed.

In case the Caledonians decided to try to force their way through by collecting a large band of raiders together, the Romans built sixteen big forts on or very near to the wall. Each of these forts would hold a complete auxiliary regiment of 500 men. Some forts were built to hold cavalry, like that shown on page 73, and so they had to be bigger than the infantry forts. Notice where the gates are – big gates on the 'enemy' side. It was not the Roman idea to wait in the forts until they were attacked, but to go out themselves on patrol and to catch anybody who looked like an enemy.

The wall was built by men of the legions, for only the legions had the technical skill to do the work. There was a big supply base near the wall, at Corstopitum (Corbridge) where the main road crossed the River Tyne, and skilled craftsmen from the legions used to make such things as armour, tools and weapons, stone shot for the catapults, harness and all sorts of equipment. The legions themselves, though, left the ordinary work of guarding the wall to the auxiliary regiments, and only came up to and beyond the wall when the northern tribes had begun a real war. Most of the time life along the wall was peaceful, and it seems that the tribes who lived anywhere near the wall soon became quite friendly; the tribes who were really dangerous were those who lived further away from the frontier, in the Highlands.

The wall was built between 122 and 128, and it was the frontier of Roman Britain for nearly 300 years. There was a short time when the Romans decided to move further north, and built another wall between the Forth and the Clyde. This was done in the reign of Emperor Antoninus Pius, who came after Hadrian, and his wall is known as the Antonine Wall.

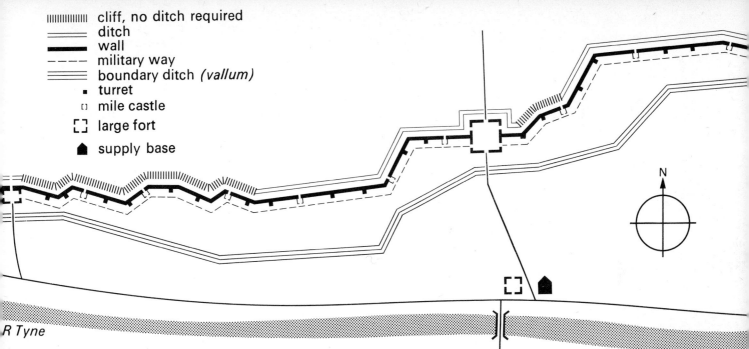

Legend

- ||||||| cliff, no ditch required
- ditch
- **wall**
- - - - military way
- boundary ditch *(vallum)*
- ▪ turret
- ◻ mile castle
- ⌞ ⌝ large fort
- ⬠ supply base

R Tyne

Schematic plan of Hadrian's Wall

But this wall proved to be too weak and too far forward, and was abandoned after forty or fifty years. Hadrian's Wall and its outpost forts held firm. Hadrian's Wall was over-run by the barbarians three times, but each time its soldiers had either gone to fight somewhere else or (on one occasion) been betrayed by other Roman soldiers who had gone over to the barbarians. As long as the Wall of Hadrian was properly used, it kept Roman Britain safe from the north.

This diagram will remind you of all the different parts of Hadrian's Wall, and how they all fitted together to do the job. There was also a big ditch to the south of the wall itself, which seems to have been meant as a boundary. Also, outside many of the forts there grew up small towns, where probably there lived merchants who traded with the barbarians and shopkeepers and inn-keepers who sold to the soldiers. There would be farmers, too.

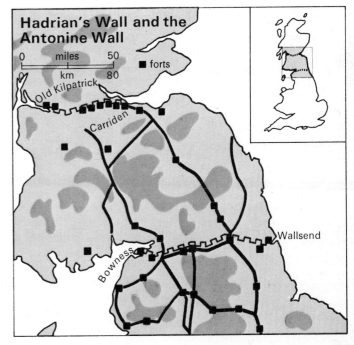

Hadrian's Wall and the Antonine Wall

0 — miles — 50
0 — km — 80

■ forts

Old Kilpatrick
Carriden
Bowness
Wallsend

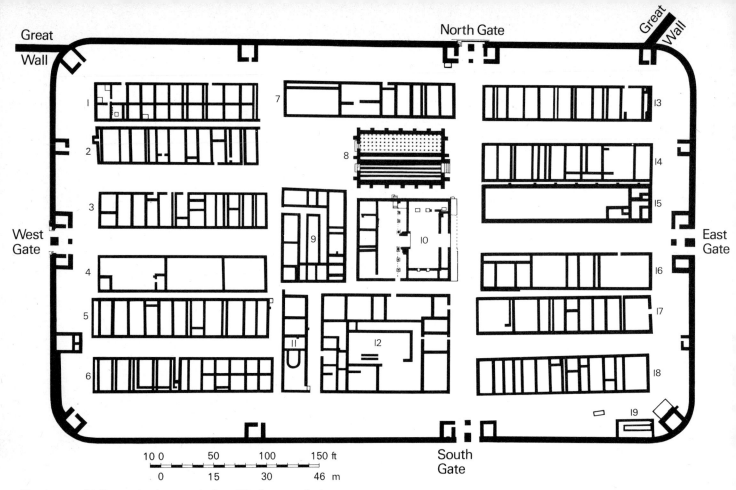

Housesteads Fort: air view and simplified ground plan. Excavations continue to reveal more details, but the typical Roman fort plan is quite clear — gates, roads, rows of barracks, main buildings in the middle.

1 - 6   Barrack blocks, with surplus space probably used for stabling and later as workshops also. Much rebuilding took place during the long life of this fort.

7   Use not certainly known. Perhaps more barracks.

8   The granaries: there were two buildings made from one big one. The patterns on the plan indicate the pillared base which allowed free circulation of air under the floor.

9   The hospital, which included a medical store and an operating theatre as well as wards.

10   The headquarters building. Here were the operations room, where orders were given; the fort chapel, where the standards were kept; the clerk's departments; the unit's savings bank; and the officers' clubs.

11   The bath-house for the commandant and his household. The men's bath-house was, as usual, outside the fort, near a stream.

12   The commandant's house, consisting of four ranges of rooms round an open courtyard. Senior officers could bring their families with them, even to such a distant post as Housesteads.

13-18   More barrack blocks.

19   The latrines. Sewage was piped to a point about 100 yards from the fort, where it was probably collected for use as manure. Fresh water was perhaps pumped to the fort from a stream near by. Water was stored in large tanks placed in many parts of the fort.

The north face of Housesteads overlooks a steep drop, which explains why no ditch was dug there.

In many places the ruins of Hadrian's Wall can still be seen, and even where they have not yet been dug up you can sometimes see the marks on the ground. These marks often show up best on an air photograph, like that on the previous page.

We have talked of Roman soldiers manning Hadrian's Wall, but here we can find a good example of how people from many different nations became Romans. From the inscriptions found on stones from the forts, we know the names of many of the regiments which were there. Opposite is a list of most of them, and a map of the Roman Empire will help you to see where each regiment came from. Many of the soldiers probably settled in Britain when they retired from the army, and these regiments, like the three legions in Britain, stayed for so long that it seems likely that many of the soldiers were in fact Britons. Yet they were all soldiers of the Roman emperor and defenders of the Roman Peace.

An inscription carved by the First Cohort of Dacian infantry stationed at Birdoswald Fort, Cumberland. It shows their peculiar Dacian sword.

A proud symbol of imperial power carved by a soldier of Legion II Augusta to commemorate building work done by his legion at Halton Chesters.

A *cohort* was an infantry regiment.
An *ala* was a cavalry regiment.
Both were usually 500 strong,
sometimes 1000.

1   Cohort I Spaniards

2   Ala I Asturians
    Ala II Asturians

3   Cohort I Aquitanians

4   Cohort IV Gauls
    Cohort V Gauls

5   Cohort I Frisians

6   Cohort I Batavians

7   Cohort I Tungrians
    Ala I Tungrians

8   Cohort I Vangiones

9   Cohort II Lingonians
    Cohort IV Lingonians

10 Cohort VI Rhaetian Spearmen

11 Sabinian Ala Pannonians

12 Cohort II Dalmatians

13 Cohort I Hadrian's Own Dacians

14 Cohort I Thracians

15 Tigris Boatmen

16 Aurelius' Own Moors

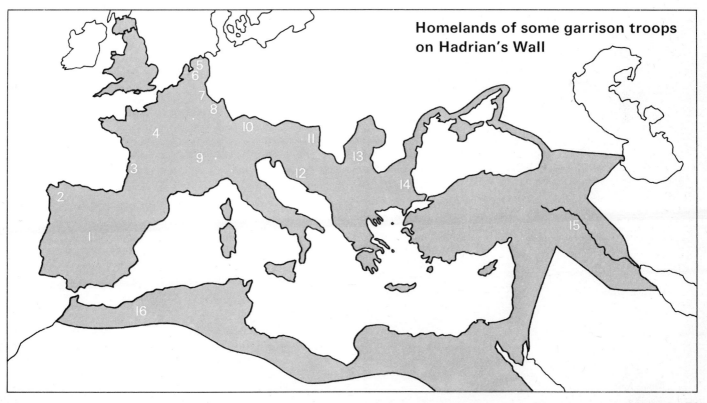

**Homelands of some garrison troops
on Hadrian's Wall**

The Saxon Shore

About 200 years after the Roman conquest of Britain, a new threat arose. This time it came from the east, across the North Sea. There came pirates from Germany, from that untamed land of forest and river and swamp beyond the Roman frontier of the Rhine. Slipping across the sea in their long, low galleys they would suddenly attack some rich place in south-east Britain, rob, kill, burn and be away before armed men could be collected to chase them. These raids were hurting the peaceful, civilized part of Roman Britain, the part that had always seemed to be so far away from the danger of barbarian raids.

To deal with this problem, the Roman government built a series of great forts around the coast. The map will show you where they were built, and the photographs will give you some idea of the strength of their walls. These forts were meant to be the bases for both soldiers and ships, so that raiders could be chased by both land and sea. This part of the coast of Britain was put under the command of a general with the title of Count of the Saxon Shore.

In spite of all this, more and more pirates seem to have thought that it was worth the risk, and the defenders of the Saxon Shore were kept busy.

For its size, Roman Britain took a lot of protecting.

left: Portchester (Portus Adurni), a Saxon Shore fort of the usual shape. The Normans built a castle in one corner, an abbey in another.

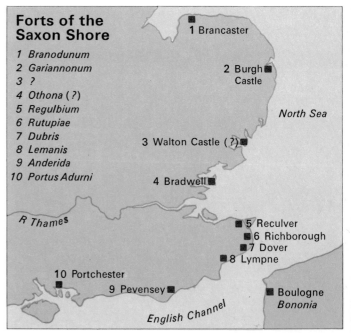

Forts of the Saxon Shore

1 Branodunum
2 Gariannonum
3 ?
4 Othona (?)
5 Regulbium
6 Rutupiae
7 Dubris
8 Lemanis
9 Anderida
10 Portus Adurni

1 Brancaster
2 Burgh Castle

North Sea

3 Walton Castle (?)

4 Bradwell

R Thames

5 Reculver
6 Richborough
7 Dover
8 Lympne

10 Portchester
9 Pevensey

Boulogne
Bononia

English Channel

above: Pevensey (Anderida), a Saxon Shore fort of unusual shape, to fit the lie of the land. During the Middle Ages a castle was built in one corner.

right: A corner of Burgh Castle (Gariannonum) with its projecting bastion. Cementing together rough stones or flints and bonding them with layers of flat bricks, as shown here, was a typical Roman building method.

The towns of Roman Britain

1 Exeter *Isca Dumnoniorum*
2 Dorchester *Durnovaria*
3 Chichester *Noviomagus Regnensium*
4 Winchester *Venta Belgarum*
5 Canterbury *Durovernum Cantiacorum*
6 Silchester *Calleva Atrebatum*
7 Bath *Aquae Sulis (spa)*
8 Caerleon *Isca Silurum (legionary base)*
9 Caerwent *Venta Silurum*
10 Gloucester *Glevum (colonia)*
11 Cirencester *Corinium Dobunnorum*
12 London *Londinium*
13 St Albans *Verulamium*
14 Colchester *Camulodunum (colonia)*
15 Wroxeter *Viroconium Cornoviorum*
16 Buxton *Aquae Arnemetiae (spa)*
17 Leicester *Ratae Coritanorum*
18 Caistor-by-Norwich *Venta Icenorum*
19 Lincoln *Lindum (colonia)*
20 Chester *Deva (legionary base)*
21 Brough-on-Humber *Petuaria*
22 York *Eboracum (legionary base & colonia)*
23 Aldborough *Isurium Brigantum*

The Roman civilization of Britain

In the areas where the soldiers were, where the land was poor and the people rough, the Britons probably went on living as they had been living before the Romans came. But in the south-east, where the land and climate were better and where it was easier to feel close to the rest of the Roman Empire, the Britons learned a great deal from the Romans.

The towns

The Romans, like most of the civilized peoples of the Mediterranean, thought that civilization went with towns and cities. A nation or tribe with no towns, but only farms and hill forts and straggling villages, simply could never be civilized. So the Romans set about teaching some of the Britons how much better it was to live in a town.

The map will show you the main towns of Roman Britain. You will see the colonies, the towns where ex-soldiers of the legions were settled, to set a good example to the Britons. Nearly all the other towns are tribal capitals. If you compare this map with the map of the British tribes on page 60 you will be able to check for yourself. You may also notice that sometimes the tribal name is in the town name.

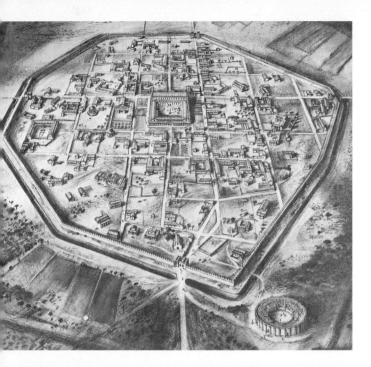

The Romans persuaded the chief men of the tribes to build houses in the towns; they even lent the Britons money and engineers to help them to do this and to lay out the streets. Then they were able to get the chief Britons to live like Romans. The Britons in the towns began to dress like Romans, to use Roman pots and pans and tools and jewels; to understand Latin, and to read and write; to go to the baths and the shows in the circus. The rich Britons became town councillors and collected the emperor's taxes and enforced the Roman law.

The only Romano-British town that has been completely excavated so far is Calleva Atrebatum (Silchester). Compare this reconstructed bird's-eye view of the town with the hill-fort on page 59, and you will see the difference that the Romans made to the lives of some of the Britons.

Another town that is being excavated is Verulamium. The pictures on the next page will give you an idea of how comfortable the houses of the richer townspeople were. The air photograph of the theatre is next to a drawing which shows you what it probably looked like when it was being used. It seems as though this theatre was designed to be used as a circus as well as an ordinary theatre of the sort that the Greeks had invented.

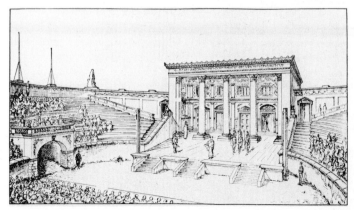

Comfort, elegance and culture

With the exception of the statuette on page 85, all these proofs of the civilization achieved in Roman Britain were found at St Albans.

Statuettes of gods and goddesses were very common. Venus, goddess of love and beauty, and one of the most popular, is shown here.

The 'Lion and Stag' mosaic floor. Reconstructed beneath it is a hypocaust, a passage for hot air, the standard Roman method of central heating.

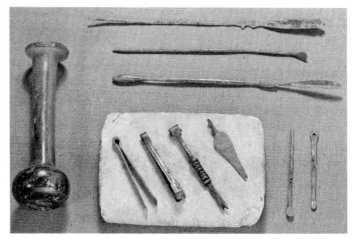

Aids to beauty. Cosmetics were kept in glass bottles, taken out with a long spoon and mixed on a fine stone palette. Tweezers, nail cleaners, ear cleaners, spatulas, probes — some of them medical instruments also — were used.

Wall plaster painted with a design of pheasants and leopards.

The 'Lion and Stag' mosaic: a closer view of the centre.

Statuette of Emperor Nero as Alexander the Great, found in Suffolk.

The countryside

The house in this picture is not a town house. It is one of the big country houses in which rich men lived in Roman Britain. We usually call such houses villas, and you can see that life in a big villa was just as civilized and luxurious as life in the town house of a rich Briton. Everything was there for the comfort of the owner and his family. You will also notice that a villa was not only a fine house to live in; it was also a farm-house, the centre of an estate. The estates in Britain were probably not as huge as those we mentioned on page 28, which belonged to rich Romans in Italy, but they seem to have been prosperous. With its workshops, stables, barns and slave-barracks as well as its fields, a big villa would be able to grow and make most of the things its people needed.

Who were the people who lived in the villas? We cannot be

left: Lullingstone Villa, Kent, as it probably looked in the fourth century AD. The left wing contained the baths, both hot and cold. The semi-circular roof which can just be seen at the back belonged to the dining room; the room was designed to allow the couches to be arranged in a half circle. In the grounds behind the villa is a square, domed temple which was also the family mausoleum. The little round building was a temple, too, perhaps for the worship of a local god of the woods.

below: A model of a British farmstead at Riding Wood, Northumberland, as it probably looked in Roman times. The countryside was better suited to raising animals than crops, and stone was the most readily available building material.

certain. Some may have been Roman officials or ex-soldiers. Most, though, were probably Britons who had become Romans.

Many of the Britons would live on these villa estates, either as owners or servants or slaves. Many more went on living on small farms that had not changed much since before the Roman invasion. Though we do not know a great deal about these farms, because not enough of them have been dug up yet, this model of one near Hadrian's Wall is probably good for most of them. Compare this with the villa, and then turn back and look at the picture of the farm on page 59. You can see where changes took place, and where they did not.

The Romans did not teach the Britons any new ways of farming; they introduced no important new tools, or crops, or farm animals. The Romans did bring peace, which allowed the Britons to enjoy their work in safety; a few water-mills were set up in some places, and some of the Fens were drained. The big changes that the Romans made were to those Britons who lived a Roman sort of life in towns and villas. In the other parts of the country the Britons went on making a living as they had before, especially in the north and the west.

Industry

Of course everything had to be made by hand, and there was nothing in the least like what we call 'industry' nowadays. Most of the articles made in Roman Britain, and which you can see in museums, would be made by craftsmen working in towns or at villas, though these men would often use Roman designs to work from. The Romans did some mining, as you can see from the map, but much of this seems to have been done by the men of the legions. There was quite a big trade in pottery. During the first hundred or so years supplies of reddish pottery called Samian Ware were brought to Britain from potteries in Gaul, but later the trade seems to have passed to British potters working in the New Forest area and at Castor, in Northamptonshire.

The map shows you where the towns and villas of Roman Britain were, the main mines and the main potteries. It will prove to you at once that there was a big difference between the north-west and the south-east of Roman Britain. Historians have spent a lot of time thinking and arguing about how far the Britons really were changed, how far they were made a different sort of people by the Romans. One thing does seem fairly clear: the people in the south-east were changed much more than the others.

A lead pig from Derbyshire, stamped with the smelter's name and the place of origin.

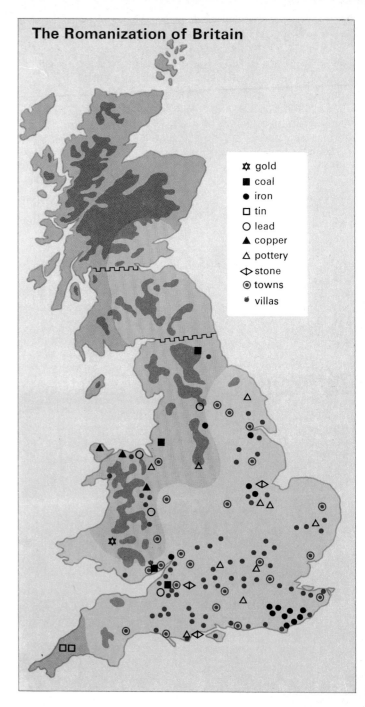

The Romanization of Britain

✪ gold
■ coal
● iron
□ tin
○ lead
▲ copper
△ pottery
◁▷ stone
◉ towns
⬤ villas

Castor ware. The swirling lines of the hunting dogs suggest Celtic art.

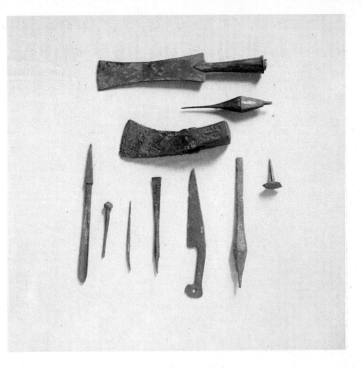

Tools once used by Romano-British tradesmen. Not much different from modern tools, chisels, awl and spoon bits for fitting to a brace, a combined hammer and axe head, a nail and a tack, a scribe and a saw, are easily identifiable.

Religion

One of the most important things that the Romans did in Britain was to bring in Christianity. After 300 years of persecution, the Christians won; a Roman emperor turned Christian, and made Christianity the most powerful religion in the Empire. That is another story, but here we can say that when the Empire broke up and all that the Romans had done in Britain seemed to be ruined, the Christian church lived on.

The world outside Rome – civilizations and barbarians

The story of Rome is such a big one that we have had space for nothing else in this book, and you may have forgotten that the Roman Empire did not include all the civilized people in the world. The first map is to remind you of the great kingdoms and empires of Asia.

The distances were so great that there was very little that the Romans or the other civilized peoples could do to help or to harm one another. Even traders found the journeys long. Trade went on. Merchants from the Roman Empire went to India, to Indo-China, even to China itself, and brought back such rare treasures as the beautiful silks which rich Romans bought.

The only civilized people near enough to the Romans to help or to harm were the Parthians, the new rulers of Persia. There were many wars between the two Empires. Border cities changed hands often. At one time Rome held Mesopotamia. But the Roman Empire was big enough already, almost too big to be ruled from one capital city like Rome. The wars between the Roman and Parthian Empires only brought harm to both sides, for both spent men and money without winning anything of lasting value, and they could not afford it.

The second map will show you why the Romans in particular could not afford to weaken themselves in useless wars with the Parthians. This map covers the same area as the last one, but instead of emphasizing the civilized peoples it shows the uncivilized peoples, the barbarians.

These barbarians were beginning to push hard at the Roman frontiers, especially on the River Danube and the River Rhine. The tribes who lived near to the Roman frontiers were being pushed by other, wilder tribes. It seemed as though so many barbarians were looking for more land to settle on, or to pasture their herds on, or just looking for more people to rob, that all the barbarian peoples were restless.

Some barbarians seem to have wanted to raid in the rich Roman Empire; others wanted to come in and settle, and be protected against the wilder barbarians outside. The Roman Empire needed to be strong to beat the first sort, and just as strong when it dealt with the second sort, because either the Romans would have to shut them out very firmly, or keep very firm control over them if they were allowed in.

During the third century A.D. the Roman Empire needed to become stronger than ever. Instead, it was beginning to weaken.

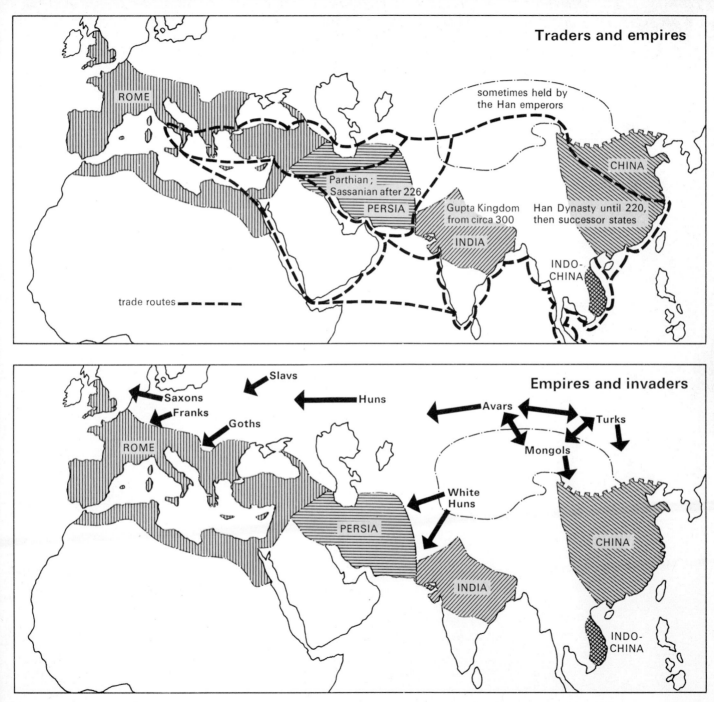

Traders and empires

ROME

sometimes held by
the Han emperors

Parthian;
Sassanian after 226

PERSIA

Gupta Kingdom
from circa 300

INDIA

Han Dynasty until 220,
then successor states

CHINA

INDO-
CHINA

trade routes ----

Empires and invaders

Slavs

Saxons

Huns

Avars

Turks

Franks

Goths

ROME

Mongols

White
Huns

PERSIA

INDIA

CHINA

INDO-
CHINA

Built between 271 and 283 to protect the city of
Rome, a large part of Emperor Aurelian's Wall still stands.
This view shows the Pincian Gate, one of the
best preserved.

below left: Part of the ruins of the baths Emperor
Caracalla built for the people of Rome in the third
century. In all the cities of the Empire, baths were not
only for washing, but more centres for leisure and
pleasure. Besides bathing rooms of all sorts, Caracalla's
baths included gymnasia, lecture rooms, libraries, music
rooms, beauty parlours and restaurants.
The reconstruction drawing of the main hall gives an
idea of the grandiose luxury some Romans enjoyed.

The Empire breaks up

The crown for sale

You remember how, when the republic broke down, the Romans at last had to accept an emperor. The idea was that a strong, wise man, in command of the army and helped by honest, hard-working officials or civil servants, would see that jobs were done promptly and well. There was one very obvious danger. What if the emperor turned out not to be strong, or not to be wise?

For a long time Rome was fairly lucky. During the second century A.D., the time of the 'Five Good Emperors' whom we mentioned on page 53, Rome was very lucky. Then the rot set in. A bad emperor was murdered. The army took over. Once the soldiers realized how strong they were, no emperor except the very strongest was safe. At one time the throne was openly sold to the Roman who would pay most. (He did not live to enjoy his crown for very long.) At other times, different armies from different frontiers each tried to make their own general the emperor. That often meant that these armies fought against each other instead of guarding the frontier, and you saw on page 75 what that could lead to. Twice Hadrian's Wall was taken by barbarians when the soldiers were away *fighting other Roman soldiers.*

Who will pay?

The army required more and more money from one emperor after another. This was, as you have just seen, partly as rewards for help or as bribes to remain loyal. It was also, though, because guarding the frontiers really was very expensive. The only way of raising the money was by making the taxes heavier.

Because the emperors did not feel safe, they felt that they had to hold the Empire very tightly. They used more officials to rule the people of the Empire, and then they had thousands of spies and secret police to watch the officials. All these cost money, too. The taxes became heavier and heavier.

Who paid the taxes? In the end, the people who paid were the people who could not dodge paying. The soldiers, the officials, the secret police, the very rich men could either dodge paying or else make up for what they paid by taking more money from somebody else. The officials and the secret police, for example, used to expect bribes.

To make things worse, all this extra demand for money came at a time when the Empire was not as prosperous as it had been, when trade was bad and when people could not afford to pay so much. You can understand that some of the people of the Roman Empire must have been wondering if it was worth it. We talked about the price that had to be paid for the Roman Peace on page 55; there was still a lot of good in the Roman Peace, but the price was very high.

Constantius Chlorus, Caesar under Maximian Augustus, is greeted by the citizens of London in 296. He has restored order after the revolt of Carausius, admiral of the British fleet, who set himself up as a rival emperor. The inscription reads, 'Restorer of Eternal Light'. This scene is on a medallion struck soon after the event.

Can the Empire hold?

After about the year 280 there were some very strong emperors. The first of these was Diocletian, the man who built that great palace which you saw on page 48. He decided that the Empire must be held firm as it was, and he ordered that everybody must stay exactly where he was. Each man would have to go on doing the same job, or the job his father was doing, and would have to go on living in the same place. If anyone ran away – taxes were so heavy that even landowners sometimes fled, leaving their farms to go to waste – his neighbours would have to take on his work and taxes as well as their own. In order to make sure that things did not change for the worse, the Emperor said that things must not change at all.

Diocletian also decided that ruling the Empire was too big a job now for one man, so he divided the Empire into east and west, with an emperor in each half. It was still supposed to be one Roman Empire, and the two emperors were to work together. What happened was that sometimes during the next hundred years the two parts came together under one emperor, and sometimes they separated.

The capital of the eastern part of the Roman Empire was Byzantium. It was so rebuilt by the Emperor Constantine that it was given a new name: Constantinople. From this great city, this new Rome of the east, an Empire was ruled for the next 1,000 years. That is a new story, and we cannot even begin it here.

Constantine did something even more important than that. He was the Roman emperor who made Christianity the religion of the whole Empire, east and west alike. In Rome itself, where so many Christians had died cruel deaths, a Christian bishop was given great honour and power. The same thing happened in all the other cities of the Empire. This was the beginning of another new story.

Big new things were happening. The story of Rome was not over. It is not over yet, and perhaps it never will be over. Think for yourself of how we are still using things, words, ideas that the Romans have left us. But in the west, the Empire began to crack into pieces. Barbarian peoples began to move in and settle in parts of the Empire. Everything got mixed up. Kingdoms sprouted up where the old provinces had been. New people were taking over, and after 476 nobody even pretended that there was an emperor in Rome.

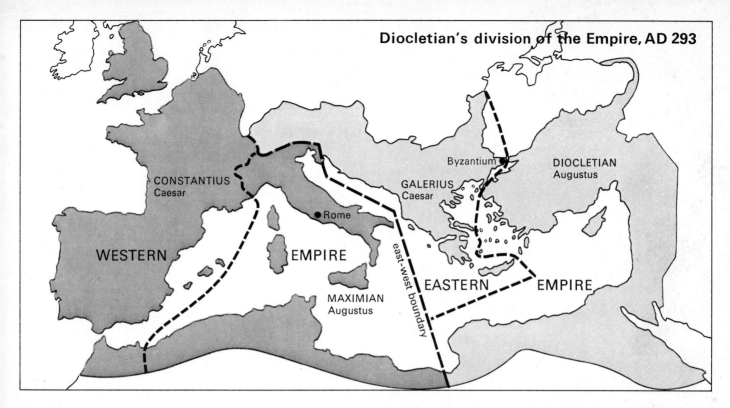

Diocletian's division of the Empire, AD 293

Maximian, titled Augustus, ruled the western Roman Empire. He looked after Italy and most of Africa himself. Constantius, titled Caesar, Maximian's heir and assistant, looked after Mauretania, Spain, Gaul and Britain.

Diocletian, who took the title of Augustus, ruled the eastern Roman Empire. He looked after Asia Minor, Syria and Egypt himself. Galerius, with the title of Caesar, was his assistant and heir. He looked after the Balkans and Greece.

There are reminders of Rome in many lands. On the next page is a photograph of the ruins at Ba'albek, in the Lebanon. The huge and ornate columns belong to the temple which Emperor Antoninus Pius built in honour of Jupiter, greatest of gods.